the
Sergeant in the Snow

MARIO RIGONI STERN

translated by
ARCHIBALD COLQUHOUN

T M P

The Marlboro Press/Northwestern
Evanston, Illinois

The Marlboro Press/Northwestern
Northwestern University Press
www.nupress.northwestern.edu

Originally published 1953 in Italian under the title *Il sergente nella neve.* Copyright © 1953 by Giulio Einaudi Editore, Turin. First published in English 1954 by MacGibbon & Kee Limited, London. First published in the United States 1967 by Alfred A. Knopf, New York. The Marlboro Press/Northwestern edition published 1998 by arrangement with Giulio Einaudi Editore S.P.A., Turin. All rights reserved.

Printed in the United States of America

10   9   8   7   6   5

ISBN-13: 978-0-8101-6055-2
ISBN-10: 0-8101-6055-2

♾ The paper used in this publication meets the minimum requirements of the American National Standard for Information Sciences—Permanence of Paper for Printed Library materials, ANSI z39.48-1992.

CONTENTS

AUTHOR'S NOTE

THE participation of Italian troops in the Russian campaign was due more to political than to military causes. The Afrika Korps had fought with the Italians in North Africa; so, just after the beginning of the German attack on Russia, Mussolini asked Hitler if he could send an Italian expeditionary force to the Russian front. This, therefore, was mainly a symbolic gesture, and, as so often happens with emotional impulses, it was to end in disaster.

The Italian Expeditionary Force (CSIR) began moving to the battle area by echelons on 10th July 1941. It consisted of about 60,000 men, and was sent to the southern part of the front, attached to the German XI Army. Even in this first phase, lack of transport forced the Italian troops to carry out exhausting marches over the muddy Ukrainian roads. From then on not only transport, but general A and Q staff-work, supply and even leave-roster services showed themselves increasingly defective.

After a very hard winter, and a year of offensive and defensive fighting, the CSIR had suffered serious losses, and was incorporated in the VIII Italian Army, which arrived in Russia in July 1942. The Italian forces in Russia now totalled about 230,000 men. They included three divisions of Alpini troops, specially trained for winter warfare; to one of these, the Tridentina, belonged the author of this book.

During the summer the ARMIR advanced to the Don, and occupied about 200 miles of front along the river, with the II Hungarian Army on its left, and the III Rumanian Army on its right. A Russian offensive was contained in August 1942, but in November the Russians started operations on a vast scale. The line held by the Rumanians on the left broke, and on 11th December the ARMIR was also subject to mass attack. Retreat began on 19th December. It went from the banks of the Don to the town of Shebekino, which the remains of the ARMIR reached on 31st January 1943. This retreat of about 300 miles was carried out entirely on foot, with no supplies, and at a temperature of 30–40 degrees below zero. Many of the troops, overcome by exhaustion, broke away from the column, others were cut off and captured by the Russians, others lost in the steppes.

The losses of the ARMIR were: about 90,000 missing and dead; about 45,000 frost-bitten and wounded.

I

The Strongpoint

I'VE STILL in my nostrils the smell of grease on a red-hot machine-gun. I've still in my ears and even in my brain the crunching of snow under my boots, the coughs and sneezes from Russian look-outs, the sound of dry grass swept by the wind on the banks of the Don. I've still in my eyes the stars of Cassiopeia which hung above my head every night, and the bunker props above my head every day. And when I think about it all I feel the terror of that January morning when their gun Katiuska first let off its seventy-two rocket-shells.

We were all right in our strongpoint for a few days after we arrived, and before the Russians attacked.

Our strongpoint was in a fishing village by the Don in the Cossack country. The gun-positions and trenches were cut out of an escarpment which hung over the frozen river. This escarpment sloped away to left and right until it merged into a river-bank covered with dry grass and reeds bristling amid the snow. Beyond a flat stretch to the right was Morbegno's strongpoint; beyond another on the left, Lieutenant Cenci's. Between us and Cenci, in a ruined house, Sergeant Garrone's section with a heavy machine-gun. Facing us, less than fifty yards away, on the other side of the river, the Russian strongpoint.

Where we were must have been a fine village once, but now the only remains of the houses were their brick fireplaces. Half the church had gone; and in the apse were Company Headquarters, an OP and a heavy machine-gun post. When we cut out communication-trenches through the gardens of destroyed houses, from the earth and snow came potatoes, cauliflowers, carrots, cucumbers. Sometimes these were good, and we made a vegetable soup from them.

The only animals that had remained alive in the village were the cats. No more geese, dogs, chickens or cows, just cats. Fat aggressive cats that wandered among the ruins of the houses hunting mice.

The mice were not part of the village, but they were part of Russia, of the land, of the steppe; they were everywhere. There were even mice in Lieutenant Sarpi's strongpoint that had been cut out of chalk. When we slept they came under the blankets with us to keep warm. The mice!

For Christmas I wanted to eat a cat and make myself a cap from its fur. I put a trap out too, but they were sly and didn't let themselves get caught. I could have killed one with a rifle shot, but it's a bit late to think of that now. I must have been really fixed on catching one in a trap for I never ate cat's meat with polenta and never made myself a cap from its fur. When we came back from sentry-go we used to grind up rye, and warm ourselves with it before going to bed. The grinder was made of two short oak trunks with long nails hammered in between. The rye was poured in above through a hole in the middle and the ground rye came out through another hole on the side of the nails. A lever turned it. In the evening before the patrols went out, hot polenta was ready. God! How hard it was, done in the Bergamese manner, and it smoked away on a real trencher made by Moreschi. I'm sure it was better than the polenta they make at home. Sometimes the Lieutenant, who was from the Marches, also came to eat it. 'How good this polenta is!' he used to say, and eat two huge hunks as big as bricks.

As we had two sacks of rye and two grinders, on Christmas Eve we sent one grinder and one sack over to Lieutenant Sarpi with our best wishes to the machine-gunners from our platoon who were up in his strongpoint.

We were all right in our bunker. When they called us on the telephone and asked: 'Who's speaking?' Chizzarri, the Lieutenant's batman, used to reply: 'Campanelli!' which was the code word for our strongpoint, named after an Alpino from Brescia who had died in September. From the other end of the wire they'd reply: 'Valstagna here; Beppo speaking.' Valstagna is the name of a village on the Brenta, ten minutes away from my home as the crow flies, but here it meant Company Headquarters. Beppo, our Captain, was a native of Valstagna. We might have been up on our native hills hearing the foresters calling to each other. Particularly at night when from the Morbegno, the strongpoint on our right, patrols went out on to the river-bank to put down barbed wire, and led their mules past our trenches and shouted and cursed and knocked stakes in with mallets. They even called out to the Russians and shouted: 'Hey! *Paruschi! spacoina noci.*' The Russians would listen in stunned silence.

But after a bit we'd got familiar with things too.

One moonlight night I went out with Tourn, the Piedmontese, to search among the farthest ruined houses. We went down into those holes that are in front of every *isba*, where the Russians put their stores for the winter and their beer in summer. In one of them were three cats making love, who jumped out angrily with such glistening eyes that they gave us quite a fright. That time I found a tin of dried cherries and Tourn two sacks of rye and two chairs, and in another hole I found a fine big mirror. We wanted to take these things back, but there was a moon and the Russian sentry on the other side of the river tried to prevent our taking them away and fired on us. He may have been right, but he couldn't have used the stuff. The bullets whistled near us as if telling us: 'Get down.' We waited behind a fireplace till clouds covered the moon, then, hopping among the ruins, we reached our dugout where our comrades were waiting.

It was really fine to sit on a chair and write to one's girl, or to shave looking at oneself in the big mirror, or drink, in the evening, the juice of the dried cherries boiled in snow water.

A pity I never managed to catch that cat.

We had to be careful about the oil for the lamps. But we had to have some light in the dugout all the time in case of an alarm, though we always had our rifles and ammunition within arm's reach.

One night when it was snowing I went out with our Lieutenant beyond our wire to the abandoned stretch of land between us and the Morbegno. There was no one there. Only the ruins of some vehicle. We wanted to see if there was anything good among these ruins. We found a drum of oil, and thought it might be useful for the lamps and for oiling our weapons. So I went back with Tourn and Bodei another night when it was dark and stormy. As we propped the drum up so's to empty it into the cans we had with us, it made a noise. The sentry fired, but it was as dark as the bottom of a polenta pot; he must have fired just to warm his hands. Bodei cursed under his breath so as not to be heard. We were nearer the

Russians than we were to our own people. By making a number of
journeys we managed to bring nearly a hundred litres of oil back to
the dugout. We gave a little to Lieutenant Cenci for his strongpoint,
then some to Lieutenant Sarpi, then the Captain wanted some too,
and the recce squad, and even the Major commanding the battalion.
Finally we got tired of being asked and replied we hadn't any more.
When the order came to retreat we left some for the Russians. In our
dugout we had three lamps made of empty meat-tins. For the wicks
we used pieces of boot leather cut into strips.

To us night was the same as day. When I went from one sentry-post
to the other I used to walk outside the communication-trenches. It
amused me to go along without making any noise and come up
behind them before they asked me, embarrassedly, for the pass-
word, 'City of Brescia.' I'd reply, then talk to them in Brescian
dialect, tell them some joke or dirty story. They'd laugh at hearing
me, a Venetian, talk their dialect. Lombardi was the only one I was
silent with. Lombardi! I can't remember his face without a shiver.
It was a dark, taciturn, gloomy face and I couldn't look at it for
long; when he smiled, which he did very rarely, it twisted my heart.
He seemed to be part of another world and to know things he
couldn't tell us. One night while I was with him, a Russian patrol
came out, and the machine-gun bullets grazed the top of the
trench. I put down my head and looked through the loophole. But
Lombardi stood up there with his whole chest exposed and never
moved an inch. I felt afraid for him, and ashamed of myself. Then
one evening during the Russian attack Sergeant Minelli came to
tell me that Lombardi had been killed by a bullet through the forehead, while he was standing outside the trench, holding and firing
a machine-gun. I remembered then how taciturn he had always
been and the feeling of vague oppression I had in his presence. As
if death were already part of him.

How funny our men were when they brought the barbed-wire cages
down in front of our trenches. I remember an Alpino, an active little
man with a thin beard, one of the best shots in Pintossi's section.
They called him 'The Duce'. He had a way of swearing all his own,
and looked ridiculous because he wore a white overshirt longer than

himself, so that it always got entangled in his boots as he walked, when he let out a string of oaths that even the Russians could hear. It also often got entangled among the barbed-wire cages which he was carrying with another man and then he swore at everything without drawing breath; home, barbed wire, post, base troops, Mussolini, his girl and the Russians. Listening to him was better than a play.

Christmas Day came along.

I knew it was Christmas Day because the Lieutenant had come into the dugout the night before to tell us: 'It's Christmas tomorrow!' I also knew because I'd received a lot of cards from Italy with trees and babies all over them. A girl had sent me one with a crib in relief, and I nailed that to one of the dugout props. We knew it was Christmas. That morning I'd just finished doing the usual round of the sentries. During the night I'd been to all the sentry-posts in the strongpoint and every time I found the guard changed I'd say: 'Happy Christmas!'

I said Happy Christmas even to the communication-trenches, to the snow, the sand, the ice on the river, even to the smoke coming out of the dugouts, even to the Russians, to Mussolini, to Stalin.

It was morning. I was standing in a forward post above the icy river and looking at the sun coming up behind the oak-woods above the Russian positions. I looked down along the river from where it appeared at a curve to where it vanished round another curve. I looked at the snow and the tracks of a hare on it; they went from our strongpoint to the Russian one opposite. 'If only I could catch that hare!' I thought. I looked around everywhere and said, 'Happy Christmas!' It was too cold to be standing there and I went up the trench and re-entered my dugout. 'Happy Christmas,' I said. 'Happy Christmas!'

Meschini was grinding the coffee in his helmet with the handle of his bayonet.

Bodei was boiling up the lice.

Giuanin was crouching in his corner near the stove.

Moreschi was mending his socks.

The ones who'd been on the last guard were asleep. There was a strong smell inside there; of coffee, dirty vests and pants boiling with the lice, and lots of other things. At midday Moreschi sent for our supplies. But as they weren't Christmas rations we decided to make polenta. Meschini fanned up the fire, and Bodei went to wash out the pot in which he'd boiled the lice.

Tourn and I had always wanted to sieve the rye-grounds, and one day, I can't remember how or when, Tourn managed to find a sieve. But what with husks and bits of whole grain, more than half the grounds stayed in the sieve, so we decided by majority vote not to sieve it any more. The polenta was hard and good.

It was Christmas afternoon. The sun was beginning to go off behind the rise and we were in our dugout smoking and chatting. Then the chaplain of the regiment came in. 'Happy Christmas, lads. Happy Christmas!' And he leant his back against one of the props, 'I'm tired,' he said, 'I've been round all the dugouts in the battalion. How many more are there after yours?'

'Only one section,' I said. 'Then there's the Morbegno.'

'Say your rosaries this evening and then write home. Be calm and happy and write home. Now I'm going on to the others. Goodbye.'

'Haven't you even a packet of Milit[1] to give us, padre?'

'Ah, yes! Here.'

And he threw down two packets of Macedonia[1] and went out. Meschini swore. Bodei swore. Giuanin said from his niche: 'Quiet, it's Christmas today!' Meschini swore more than ever: 'Always Macedonia,' he said, 'and never any tobacco or Popolari[1] or Milit. These are just straw for young ladies.'

'Curse it,' said Tourn, 'Macedonia.'

'Hell,' said Moreschi, 'Macedonia.'

Then as it was getting dark I sent out the first pair of sentries. I was standing there scratching my back near the stove when Chizzarri came in and called me: 'Sergeant-major,' he said, 'you're wanted on the telephone. It's the Captain.' I put on my greatcoat and took up my rifle, asking myself if I'd done anything wrong. The telephone was in the Lieutenant's dugout. The Lieutenant was out, perhaps walking along the river-bank listening to the sneezes from the Russian posts.

It was the Captain himself, Beppo, wanting me to go up to Val-

[1] Cigarettes.

stagna, to Company Headquarters. He had something to tell me. 'What can it be?' I thought, as I went up to the ruined church.

The Captain was waiting for me, his face round and red, in his wide comfortable dugout. He had his cap on one side, its feather sticking up like a coxcomb, and his hands in his pockets. 'Happy Christmas!' he said. Then he held out his hand and offered me a glass of milk with brandy in it. He asked me how things were at home and at our strongpoint, then thrust a flask of wine and two packets of spaghetti into my arms. I went skipping back through the snow like a young goat in spring-time. In my excitement I slipped and fell but didn't break the bottle or lose the spaghetti. It's all a matter of how one falls. Once I slipped on the ice with four mess-tins full of wine and never spilt a drop; even down on the ground I'd kept the mess-tins level on my outstretched arms. But it was only in Italy, at the ski-ing course that I ever had four mess-tins full of wine.

When I reached the strongpoint and the sentries called, 'Halt-who-goes-there-pass-word,' I shouted out so loudly that the Russians must have heard me too: 'Wine and spaghetti!'

One day when I was lying stretched on the straw looking up at the props and wondering what new things I could think of to write to my girl, Chizzarri came to tell me that Lieutenant Cenci had telephoned for me to go and talk to him. I went off along the trench leading to his strongpoint.

I might have been back home going from one village to another to visit a friend and have a chat at the tavern. But it was different at Lieutenant Cenci's. He had a white dugout scooped out of chalk, while ours were black. Inside there was a well-made bed, with clean sheets without a wrinkle in them, a table with a blanket over it, some books, and a petrol lamp that looked like an ornament. Near the entrance, in a niche, was a row of red and black hand-grenades that might have been flowers. Propped against the wall near the bed was his gleaming rifle; next to it his helmet hanging on a hook. Not a straw or cigarette end on the floor. Before I entered I banged and scraped my boots so as not to bring any snow in.

Lieutenant Cenci, smiling, was standing waiting for me in his clean uniform with his white balaclava twisted round his head like an Indian turban. He asked after my girl, we talked about pleasant things, and then he called his batman to make coffee for us. When I was going he gave me a packet of Africa[1] and lent me a book about an airman who flew over the oceans, the Andes and the desert. He came with me round the posts in his strongpoint; looking at his machine-guns' field of fire I mentioned that they ought to aim a little higher and to the left because the bullets passed over our trench and we couldn't put our noses outside, as had once happened when they were firing at a Russian patrol that came near us.

As I went back alone to my dugout I wondered if I'd find any mail and what new things I'd write to my girl. But the new things were always the same as the old ones; kisses, love, I'll be back. They'd never understand a word, I thought, if I wrote: a cat for Christmas, oil for the weapons, sentry-go, Beppo, gun-sites, Lieutenant Moscioni, Corporal Pintossi, barbed wire; no, they'd never understand a word.

Tourn, the Piedmontese, was gayer than any of us, though a bit timid. They'd sent him to our battalion as a punishment because he'd come back late from leave. He wasn't happy with us at first, but later became very much so. When he'd get back to the dugout, after his turn on sentry-go, he'd shout in dialect: 'Waitress, bring a flask of wine!'

Bodei, who was a Brescian like all the others, would reply also in dialect:

'Black or white?'

'Any wine,' replied Tourn, and then sang: 'In the shade of a little bush . . .'

One day I asked him: 'Tourn, have you had any mail from home?' 'Yes,' he said, 'I've already smoked it all.'

For Tourn used to gather up all the cigarette butts, take the tobacco out and use the airmail letters he got from home as cigarette papers. So he saw to it that from home they always wrote to him on airmail paper and always had something to smoke.

Giuanin, on the other hand, had a habit of calling me aside almost every time I met him, winking and whispering in dialect: 'Sergeant-major, shall we ever get home?'

[1] Cigarettes.

For he was quite convinced I knew how the war would end, who'd be alive then, who'd die and when. So I used to reply firmly: 'Yes, Giuanin, we'll get home.' He also expected me to know if he'd marry his girl. Sometimes I'd reply that he ought to be careful of the stay-at-homes.

He'd crouch down in his niche near the stove and even his eyes seemed to repeat: 'Sergeant-major, shall we ever get home?' It was as if we two had a secret between us.

Meschini was a fine lad too. It was he who made the polenta in the evening. He used to mix it with great energy, his shirt sleeves rolled to the elbow, a drop of sweat on every hair in his beard. He'd splay his legs out, and one could see the muscles of his arms and face go taut. That's how Meschini mixed the polenta, looking like Vulcan at his anvil. He used to tell us that when he was in Albania the strain turned the hair of the black mules white and the mud made the white mules black. Those with only a few months' service used to listen to him incredulously. He was an ex-mule driver and still smelt of it; his beard was like mule hair, his strength mulish, the war had made him like a mule, even the polenta he mixed was mule food. He was earth coloured, as we all were.

Lieutenant Moscioni who commanded the strongpoint was like us. He too worked and rested like a mule, cutting communication-trenches with us during the day and going with us at night to carry down barbed wire in front of our trenches, making gun-sites, taking poles from ruined houses, and eating polenta like mule food.

But he had something we hadn't; in his pack he kept packets of Popolari and Milit cigarettes which he smoked secretly in his dug-out; though to us he only gave Macedonia, which were like smoking potato peel. Moreschi, the corporal in charge of the 45 mm. mortar, tried to exchange Macedonia for Milit but the Lieutenant wouldn't even take two for one. But Moreschi seemed to get hold of Milits somehow——

On New Year's Eve we had fireworks. God how cold it was! The constellations of Cassiopeia and the Pleiades shone away above our heads, the river was completely iced over and we had to change the sentries every half hour.

That evening I'd accompanied the Lieutenant as far as Sergeant

Garronne's post. They were playing cards there. Outside the sentry was standing near the heavy machine-gun. The barrel was pointing towards a field of frozen maize; it looked like a goat's neck it seemed so thin; hanging under it was a helmet full of burning ash.

The sentry was scratching himself; the mules had sores and he had scabies. As we went back towards our strongpoint we might have been on our way home. The Lieutenant wanted to fire a shot with his pistol to see if the sentries were on the alert. The pistol went; click. Then I tried to fire a shot from my rifle and the rifle went; click. Finally he told me to throw a hand-grenade and the grenade didn't even go click, it just vanished into the snow without making any noise at all.

God it was cold.

Then, towards midnight, the fireworks came. Suddenly tracers split the sky, machine-gun bullets passed mewing over our strong-point and the 152 mms. burst in front of our trenches; immediately afterwards the 75/13 mms. and Baroni's 8 mm. mortars split the air and the fishes in the river. The earth shook and sand and snow fell from the trenches. Even round Brescia on San Faustino's day one never heard such a row. The stars weren't to be seen any more and the cats had all vanished somewhere. The bullets sent sparks out as they hit the barbed wire. Suddenly all went calm again, just as after the fireworks everything goes silent and the deserted streets are left to sweet-papers and bits of toy trumpets. The only sound was an occasional solitary shot or a short burst of machine-gun fire like the last guffaws of a wandering drunk looking for a tavern. The stars began to shine over our heads again and the cats to put their noses out of the ruined houses. On the Don the water began icing over the holes made by the explosions. The Lieutenant and I were watching the darkness and listening to the silence. We heard Chizzari coming to look for us. 'Lieutenant, you're wanted on the telephone, sir,' he said. I remained there alone looking at the barbed wire half buried in the snow, the dried grass on the hard silent river-bank, trying to make out the Russians' positions through the dark on the other side. Then I heard one of our sentries cough and a long muffled step like a wolf's; the Lieutenant was coming back. 'What was it?' I said. 'Sarpi's dead,' he replied. I looked into the darkness and listened to the silence again. The Lieutenant bent down in the trench, lit two cigarettes and passed me one. I felt as if I'd been kicked in the stomach, my throat seemed choked up, I wanted to be sick and couldn't. Lieutenant Sarpi. There was nothing round me any more, not even the stars, not even the cold. Only that pain in my stomach. 'It was a patrol,' said the Lieutenant; 'it broke into his trenches from the rear. He ran out of his dugout and got a machine-gun burst in the chest at the bend of a communication-trench. They've also captured one of the company drivers who was clearing away snow. Now let's go and sleep. Happy New Year to you, Rigoni.' We shook hands.

I went to sleep at dawn like every morning; I lay down as usual on straw which had once roofed an *isba*, with my boots, pouches and balaclava on; I pulled up my overcoat with its fur lining and fell asleep looking at the bunker props. As usual, towards ten Giuanin woke me to distribute the rations. They were special ones that morning; potatoes in sauce, meat, cheese and wine; they'd frozen as they always did on the way from the kitchens. Seeing the special rations reminded me it was New Year's Day and that Lieutenant Sarpi had died during the night. I left the dugout. The sun made everything seem white; I went slowly along the trenches towards the most advanced positions near the barbed wire. From there I looked at the tracks of the Russian patrol which had crossed the river a hundred yards from us. Everything was silent. The sun beat down on the snow, Lieutenant Sarpi had died in the night from a machine-gun burst in the chest. Now the oranges are ripening in my garden at home, but he died in a dark trench. His old mother will get Christmas greetings from him. This morning his men will carry him down on a stretcher towards the rear and put him in a cemetery, a Sicilian among Brescians and Bergamese. You were pleased with your machine-gunners, Lieutenant; even if they swore when you ordered them to clean their weapons and you didn't like swearing. You used to come to our dugout in the evening. First we said the rosary, then we sang, then we swore. In the end you used to laugh, Lieutenant Sarpi, and even produce a few coarse words in Sicilian dialect yourself. Now a hundred yards away are the tracks of the patrol. You often used to talk about my home parts, looking at me fixedly with those small black eyes of yours. When Giuanin asked Lieutenant Sarpi: 'When shall we ever get home, Lieutenant?'

he'd say, 'In '48, Giuanin, in '48.' Giuanin would wink, drop his head gloomily back down between his shoulders, and go off muttering. The Lieutenant would laugh, call him and give him a Popolare.[1] Last night the Russian patrol passed there and he died, with the snow coming into his mouth and the blood oozing out slower and slower until it froze on the snow.

In his niche near the stove Giuanin will be eating his rations and thinking: 'Shall we ever get home?'

I walked along the trenches alone, stopped near a sentry and said nothing; then looked through a loophole at the snow on the river; the tracks of the patrol couldn't be seen any more, but I felt them inside me and still do, like little shadows on the icy light of the snow.

I went towards Baffo's section on the extreme right. This post was the calmest and safest in the whole position, set where the village straggled off into thickets and orchards. Over there they were preparing a position for the heavy machine-gun and Lieutenant Moscioni and I had worked for hours at night arranging the sandbags. One evening in an *isba* that was almost intact we found an anchor, a strange tool to us men from the mountains, and that little one-roomed house became the fisherman's *isba* for us. As I walked along I thought of this fisherman; where was he now? I imagined him as old and large, with a white beard like Uncle Jeroska in Tolstoy's *Cossaks*. How long ago had I read that book? When I was a boy at home. And Lieutenant Sarpi died last night. 'What's the matter, Sergeant-major?' 'Isn't it a fine sunny day?' 'Happy New Year, Sergeant-major.' 'Happy New Year, Marangoni.' 'What direction is Italy in, Sergeant-major?' 'Over there, you see? A long way over there. The earth is round, Marangoni, and we're among the stars. All of us.'

Marangoni looked at me, understood and was silent. And now Marangoni's dead too, with so many others. He was always laughing, and when he got any mail would wave the letter at me. 'It's from my girl,' he'd say. And now he's dead too. One morning when he had come off guard at dawn, he climbed up on top of the trench to get some snow to make coffee. There was a single rifle shot and he dropped down into the trench with a hole in his temple. He died

[1] Cigarette.

shortly afterwards in his dugout among his comrades and I hadn't
the heart to go and see him. We'd all gone out like that at dawn so
often, I too a number of times, and no one had fired. The Russians
used to come out too and we never fired at them. Why was there a
shot that morning? And why did Marangoni die like that? Perhaps
the Russians had changed over during the night and these were
new ones. 'Be careful to go out with your helmets on,' I said in the
various dugouts. I felt like settling down with a rifle and waiting for
the Russians as one waits for hares. But did nothing.

The dugout of Baffo's section was the smelliest and untidiest in the
strongpoint. When one first entered one couldn't make anything
out. There was a thick mist, heavy with innumerable smells; I
could hear muttered words and the shouts of two Alpini quarrelling
for the pot where the lice were boiled. 'Good morning and Happy
New Year to you all!' I shouted at the entrance. And with me came
a breath of cold white air. Someone replied, another held out a hand
to me, another grumbled away between his teeth. Little by little I
began to distinguish moving figures. I made peace between the two
quarrelling over the pot. Talking in their dialect, I told them about
the patrol and about Lieutenant Sarpi's death. I knew Baffo was
listening to me though he was pretending to sleep. He didn't much
like seeing me in his dugout. He used to criticize me to his men,
some of whom believed him and some not. I was very sorry at this
happening in our strongpoint where we all worked together and
helped each other mutually. He couldn't stand me because I used
to call him up at night to make sure he'd changed his sentries, and
because I told him to keep his weapons clean and his dugout tidy.
He used to complain when the mail didn't arrive, when the rations
were scanty, when it was cold, when there was smoke, when there
was dysentery, always. Then if the mail did arrive he wasn't content, and if the stove didn't smoke he wasn't content, if the rations
were enough he wasn't content, nor if the lice left him in peace, nor if
it was warm. The men of his section did half the work of those of
Pintossi's. They took days and days to make a position, and one
had to be there urging them on and working hard with them as an
example. They were also afraid of crossing the empty part down
between us and the Morbegno strongpoint. Pintossi's men, on the

other hand, had even made a stove-pipe from tins wedged on top of each other. Baffo was like that because he was tired of being in the army. He was over thirty and had spent about eight years doing military service; he'd been in Africa, then drawn lots for Spain, then in Albania and finally here. He'd come to our company with reinforcements in the first of September. And he was tired of the army, he couldn't stand it any more.

I talked loudly in their dialect so that Baffo should hear me. I talked about their children, asked who had any, and what was the way to their homes, and promised I'd come and visit them as a civilian. I talked about how we'd get drunk together, and how we'd sing as we drank the new wine. To one I said: 'Look out, there's a row of lice on your neck.' Then they laughed and another one said to me: 'Sergeant-major, you've got a patrol of them coming out of your sleeve, they've got a hammer and sickle on their backs, look out for the Russian ones!' Then I laughed, and everyone laughed. Baffo was still pretending to sleep. Before I left I went towards him, called him and held out my hand. 'Happy New Year; you'll see we'll be home one day and get drunk together.' 'It's endless, it's endless,' he replied.

So we spent the days; in our dugouts writing or thinking as we looked at the props, or throwing lice on to the red-hot top of the stove; they'd go white all over and then explode. At night we went out to listen to the silence or look at the stars, prepare gun-sites, plant barbed wire, and pass from one sentry-post to another. A lot of nights we spent cutting brushwood and bamboo in front of Pintossi's positions. How strange it was to cut brush and plants with hatchets and bayonets, beyond the barbed wire, on cold nights in the snow! One could feel that the Russians were being quiet so as to listen to what we were doing. We'd pile all the undergrowth we'd cut into a great heap in front of us. They made a fine big obstacle, even more difficult to cross than the barbed wire. And noisier.

When it snowed we had to keep very careful look-out for sudden raids. One night while I was going round with my white shirt over my overcoat, like a ghost, I noticed a Russian patrol trying to slip round under the strongpoint. I couldn't see the Russians but felt their presence a few paces from me. I stood silent and still. And they were silent and still. I felt they were looking round in the dark as I was, their weapons at the ready. I was so frightened I almost began trembling. What if they captured and took me away? I tried to control myself but the veins in my throat were throbbing hard. I really was frightened. Finally I made up my mind; I shouted, threw the grenades I had in my hand, and jumped down into the trench. Luckily one of the grenades went off. I heard the Russians running and by the flash saw them retreating into the nearest bushes. From there they opened fire with a machine-gun. Meanwhile some of Pintossi's men had arrived. We began to fire too from the top of the trench. One of us hurried off to get the machine-gun. We fired it and then moved it a few yards. The Russian patrol replied to our fire but slowly drew farther back. Then they stopped some way off and began firing continuously with a heavy machine-gun. But eventually it got too cold, they went back to their dugouts and we to ours. If they'd been able to capture one of us they might have been sent home on leave. In the morning, in sunlight, I went out to look at the tracks they'd left. They'd been farther away than I'd supposed the night before, and I smoked a cigarette and looked at their positions on the other side of the river. Every now and again one of them got up to take snow from the top of the trench. They'll be making tea, I thought. I felt I'd like a little cup too. And I looked at them as one looks at a peasant scattering manure in the fields.

Some time after I heard that I'd been proposed for a medal because of that night. I really don't know what I did to deserve it.

At the beginning of January three infantry soldiers arrived at our strongpoint with the rations. They were southerners from the Vicenza Division which the higher command had decided to break up, for some reason or other, and scatter its men among the Alpini companies. Our Lieutenant assigned them to Baffo's section.

In the evening I went to visit them. Two of them didn't want to go out on sentry-go; they didn't dare, they told me in their dialect, and one of them cried. I got two Alpini to go with them to the sentry-post, and then to convince them there wasn't any danger I walked along the top of the trench and as far as the ruins, whistling as I went, and certain that the Russians wouldn't fire. I thought I'd convinced them, but they refused to stay there alone, so I had to put an Alpino with them. The third man, on the other hand, was all right. He'd been a conjurer in a circus, knew any number of tricks, and kept everyone in his dugout happy with them and with jokes which made even Baffo laugh. The Alpini took to him a lot. He could even play tunes with two pieces of wood against his teeth, and quickly learnt to play the Alpini songs that way.

When I told Moreschi about this he replied: 'Have you ever seen a seven-hundredweight goat?' For Moreschi never believed anything and when someone told him he had a prettier girl than anyone else or a packet of fifty cigarettes in his pack or a demijohn of wine at home waiting for his return, he'd suddenly come out with: 'Have you ever seen a seven-hundredweight goat?' Every now and again he'd tell the story of the man who stopped the Orient Express at Brescia. He was sitting with friends in the middle of the railway line when he felt a push at his back, and turned round angrily shouting: 'Who's pushing me?' and found it was the Orient Express coming from Milan. 'But,' added Moreschi, 'he was a corporal in the heavies, with great wide shoulders.' Then he looked at the new recruits and repeated: 'Have you ever seen a goat that weighs seven hundredweight?' his lips opening and showing a row of white teeth between his thick black moustache and beard; under their lids his eyes had a simple kindly smile. Meschini stopped stirring the polenta and, glancing at the recruits too, commented: 'He wasn't a corporal in the heavies, but in the mortars.' And the recruits laughed.

Towards the tenth of January bad news began arriving with the rations. Tourn and Bodei, who had been to the kitchens, said they'd heard from the drivers that we'd been surrounded for some days. More gossip reached us every day; the Alpini began to feel nervous. They'd ask me what direction Italy was in and how many miles away. Giuanin asked me more and more often: 'Sergeant-major, shall we ever get home?' I too felt something was wrong. The Russians beyond the river had changed over and were working away at night cutting brushwood and thickets to widen their field of fire. When I was alone I'd look down towards the south where the river turned and see flashes like summer lightning. But they were faint and seemed to come from beyond the stars. Sometimes when all was silent I'd hear a distant sound like wheels crunching over flints. The noise seemed to fill the night. But I said nothing to the sentries, who must have heard it themselves. The Russians had become more active, and I went round with a rifle at the ready under my arm and one of the better type of grenades in my hand. The mail and the rations still arrived regularly.

One evening when I was in the Lieutenant's dugout smoking a cigarette and we were alone, 'Rigoni,' he said, 'I've had instructions in case of retreat.' I didn't reply, but I realized it was all up now, really up, though I didn't want to admit it. I felt that pain in the stomach I'd had before. I understood our own position and what the Russians were after. As I went back to my dugout I said out loud: 'Whatever happens always remember that we must stick together.'

The Lieutenant wanted to have all the automatic weapons tested and our dugout had become a workshop. Moreschi, who as a civilian had been an armourer in a factory at Valtrompia, was cleaning, oiling, dismembering the weapons, and even retempering the springs to adapt them more to the cold. When a weapon was ready it was taken along the trenches towards Baffo's section. There I would fire it, while Moreschi and the Lieutenant listened and watched how it worked. Sometimes Moreschi wasn't satisfied, he'd scratch his head and purse his lips, then take the weapon back to the dugout and begin all over again. When they were all ready he advised me to tell the section commanders to keep them well wrapped up in blankets against the cold and in pieces of tent against the fine sand which filtered into the dugout and penetrated everywhere. Finally, after a great deal of work and encouragement, the four machine-guns, the heavy machine-gun, and the four 45 mm. mortars were in perfect working order.

One of these last evenings a small Russian patrol crept under our barbed wire and, passing unobserved under the escarpment, reached the sentry-post where, luckily, Lombardi was on duty. He threw some hand-grenades, the third of which exploded, fired a shot or two, and the Russians, seeing they'd been spotted, retreated. As soon as I heard the grenades and the shots I ran towards him. He said, as if he were talking about a herd of cows: 'A Russian patrol's been here; one of them was dragging a sort of cart and leaving a trail of wire behind. They must have been a couple of yards away from here.' I didn't say anything, not wanting to believe him, and after a bit went on to the other posts. Next morning, when the sun came up, I saw tracks right up to where Lombardi had said, and felt ashamed of not having believed him. He'd been so calm and impassive!

Something was really wrong; we were all living in a state of tension and the Lieutenant took very little rest; he was always going round from one post to another, day and night. When one night he thought he heard sounds under our escarpment he lay stretched out on the snow with two grenades ready, until he was almost numbed. And it wasn't anything; a hare or a cat perhaps.

An Alpino from my own squad, A——, couldn't take it any more; he'd come back from hospital a short time before, had scabies, and was determined to become a cook. One morning I'd gone into the dugout and just laid down on the straw, when he gently turned the safety catch on my rifle, which I'd hung by a nail on one of the props, and then, as he was talking to the others, pulled the trigger; his foot was under the barrel. But he'd aimed badly and only hit the top of his boot. I didn't say anything, but just looked at him and let him realize I'd guessed what he was up to. The day after, when he was alone and just about to go out to take his turn on sentry-go, his rifle, according to his account, fired a shot which went right through his foot. The Lieutenant had him taken to hospital, no one guessed the truth. Two days later, during the Russian attack, I talked to the Lieutenant about this. 'You see,' I said, 'he couldn't stand it here any longer; he was too frightened.' Now this man is probably living peacefully at home and drawing a pension.

Corporal Pintossi was perhaps the best of all of us; what a good game-shot he was! And what a passion he had for it! He looked short because he had wide shoulders and a bit of a paunch. His small sharp eyes were always smiling. Careless about his clothes, he carried his rifle with the ease and familiarity of the born sportsman. He was calm and phlegmatic, and I never saw him annoyed and never heard him swear. And he was always present at the moment of need, placidly holding his inseparable rifle. What a good shot he was! He very seldom gave orders to his section but did things himself and his men followed his example. I often talked to him about hunting game. 'Quail shooting's the best sport. When we get back to Italy we'll go out together. I've got a dog at home that's really first-rate.' He crooked his finger: 'He's called Dirk. What a fine beast.' When he talked about his dog he'd get sad.

The other corporal in the section was called Gennaro. I don't know exactly where he came from, but he was certainly a southerner. A schoolmaster or accountant or something of the sort, he'd done an officer's course. But he hadn't been thought good enough and so became a corporal. He didn't talk much, was timid with the Alpini who, although they teased him sometimes, felt respect and affection for him. He certainly had no lion's heart but his personality, unconsciously, affected all who lived near him. There were never any quarrels in his squad about dividing the rations or taking turns at sentry-go or work. His machine-gun was always in order. When there was an alarm or Russian patrols were about, he was among the first to leave the dugout and run towards the threatened position. And yet I'm sure that inside himself he was trembling like a birch-leaf.

Eventually one morning before dawn the Russians began firing mortars and artillery at Sarpi's strongpoint, then at Cenci's, and then lengthened their range towards the kitchens, and then on to our Company Headquarters. They couldn't fire at us, I thought, as we were too near them. The men in the dugout looked at each other in silence, their rifles between their knees, their pockets and pouches full of hand-grenades under the white overshirts. I tried to make jokes but the smiles soon died away in their long dirty beards. No one was thinking, 'I may die'; but all of us felt an anguished sense of oppression and we were all thinking: 'How many miles have we to go before getting home?'

Our artillery began to answer the Russian fire and we no longer felt so alone. The shells passed so close over our heads that it seemed we could touch them if we raised a hand. They exploded on the river in front of us, on the Russian positions and in the oak-woods. Sand filtered down among the props of our dugout and the snow dropped off the edge of the trenches. A couple of shells fell short into our wire and near us. I left only two sentries out in sheltered posts, and the Lieutenant sent a message for the guns to lengthen range. As soon as day broke the artillery stopped firing and the first waves of Russians began to cross the river. I expected a frontal attack on us, but instead they bore left, beyond Cenci's strongpoint. Perhaps they hoped to penetrate that part and into a valley running in there, then press on down it towards the kitchens and Headquarters.

The river was wider, down where they were crossing; in the middle of it was an island covered with vegetation and the banks on our side were swampy and dotted with little mounds and tall dry grass and shrubs. Not a touch of human hands anywhere. The Russians coming suddenly out of the oak-woods and finding themselves in the middle of that whiteness must have been dazed and blinking. They didn't shout and only fired a short burst or two as they ran crouching towards the islet in the middle of the river. One or two of them were dragging sleighs. It was a clear morning and in the light of the young sun I looked at the Russians running on the frozen river. Cenci's machine-gunners and the heavies on that side began to fire. One or two of those in the middle of the river fell. They reached the islet, stopped a bit to draw breath and then came running on towards our bank. Wounded were going slowly upwards the woods from which they'd started. The others reached our side of the river and flung themselves among the bushes and mounds. There they were sheltered from Cenci's machine-guns, but not from ours. The Lieutenant and I were watching the motionless groups in the thickets. He sent for the heavy machine-gun which was over near Baffo. We sited the gun under the barbed wire. 'It's about six hundred yards,' said the Lieutenant. I aimed and fired a round or two. But these weren't much good as the gun was wobbling on the snow; also it stuck every now and again, and wasn't easy to work on in that narrow place. But at last the bullets reached the Russians down there, for we could see them moving about in the bushes. The Lieutenant looked serious, almost sad.

Time passed and the Russians did not begin another advance; every now and again one of them would come out and run a few yards then hide again. Suddenly mortar-shells began to fall down there. They burst so exactly on their targets that they might have been laid there by hand. They were Baroni's 81 mms. and Baroni was not one to waste either shells or wine. So the first Russian attack ended. It wasn't a real proper attack; perhaps the Russians thought our morale would be much lower and that, knowing we were surrounded, we'd clear out of the strongpoint at the first sign of their advance. But we still had a sense of apprehension; as if a great weight was hanging on our backs. I read it in the eyes of the Alpini too, and saw their uncertainty and fear of being abandoned in the steppes; we no longer felt we had any communications or liaison, or stores or headquarters, only a sense of the immense distances separating us from our homes. The only reality in that desert of snow was the Russians there in front of us, ready to attack.

'Sergeant-major, shall we ever get home?' Those words were part of me now, part of my responsibility, and I tried to cheer myself by talking about girls and drinking bouts at home. There were still some among us who wrote home: 'I'm well, don't worry about me, your loving . . .' but now these too looked at me gloomily and asked, pointing to the west: 'Which way do we go in case of . . . ? What shall we take with us?' Yet no one had told them how things were, and no one imagined, I'm sure, what was ahead of us. But we felt what an animal feels when he senses an ambush.

That evening the Lieutenant called me. 'We've had orders to withdraw.' That's what he said; *withdraw*. 'We're surrounded; the Russian tanks have reached Corps Headquarters.' The Lieutenant offered me his tobacco pouch, but I wasn't capable of rolling myself a cigarette and he did it for me.

Towards nightfall the rations and the bread arrived all frozen hard as usual.

The Russian artillery and mortars began firing again. It was getting dark and the moon would soon be out. Back home at that moment they were sitting down to supper.

I never stayed long in the dugout now; I was always in the trenches up on the escarpment above the river, with my rifle and hand-grenades. Lots of things passed through my mind, I lived over all sorts of memories and the thought of those hours is dear to me. There was I in the war, in the real war, but I wasn't living in it, I was living intensely in dreams and memories which were truer than the real war. The river was frozen, the stars were cold, the snow was glass that cracked under my boots, cold green death waited down on that river, but I felt a warmth inside me which melted all that.

Both the Lieutenant and I noticed unusual noises and movement in front of us. We had the heavy machine-gun brought out and sited it among the ruins of a house a little way back, so as to have a better field of fire. The Alpini were standing silently in the trenches. Now was the time when we ourselves should attack. Would the weapons function in that cold? Out there could be heard the sound of engines. Then came a strange silence, the kind of silence that precedes serious events. Nothing existed but the objects around us and the anxiety of the moment.

A voice was heard shouting incitement, then they came out to the assault. They appeared on the escarpment above the river, sat on the snow and slid down to the river-bank. Our guns opened fire. I breathed a sigh of relief; they worked. Moreschi's 45 mm. mortars were firing in front of our wire and their bombs burst with an odd rather absurd noise. When I heard the bombs of Sergeant Baroni's 81 mm. mortars pass over our heads, I breathed another sigh of relief. I imagined Baroni looking down towards us and placidly giving his fire-orders to his men, as if he were saying: 'Keep calm now, I'm here too.' And Baroni wasn't one ever to waste a word.

The Russians ran, threw themselves down on the ground, got up again and began running towards us once more. But many didn't get up; the wounded called and screamed. The others shouted: 'Hurrah! Hurrah!' and came on. But they didn't manage to reach our wire. I felt safe then; I could still go on living in my dugout and reading my love letters. I didn't think of the tanks which had already reached Corps Headquarters, nor how many miles there were to reach home. I felt calm and fired my rifle from the top of the trench, taking careful aim at those who were nearing us. And then I began to sing in Piedmontese dialect: 'In the shadow of a bush slept a pretty shepherdess.' Chizzarri, the Lieutenant's batman who was beside me, stopped firing and looked at me in surprise; then as he began firing again he sang with me too. In the moonlight I could make out the faces of the Alpini, relaxed and smiling. I saw that they were firing calmly; the one with the thick bristly beard changed, swearing as he did so, the red-hot barrel of the machine-gun, then went on firing intensely. The Russians soon realized that it was impossible to pass through us and moved farther over to the left, where they managed to infiltrate into the little valley between us and Cenci. They hid themselves among the bushes and shadows and it was difficult to make them out. A minefield was supposed to be there but no mine exploded. One or two Alpini went back to the dugout to fetch ammunition and hand-grenades. But we had almost finished our ammunition. During the attack, when the Russians had reached our wire, we had thrown nearly a case full of hand-grenades. But few of them went off; they buried themselves in the snow without a sound. Then it occurred to me that they might go off if both the safety pins were taken out before throwing them, and I did this, though it was rather dangerous.

Silence fell again. A burst or two of machine-gun fire could be heard between us and Cenci.

The wounded were lying on the iced river and dragging themselves along moaning. I heard one of them calling out hoarsely: '*Mama! Mama!*'

By his voice he seemed a boy. He was moving a little on the snow and sobbing. 'Just like one of us,' said an Alpino, 'he's calling his mother.'

The moon was rushing through the clouds; now nothing seemed to exist any more but laments. '*Mama! Mama!*' the boy on the river called and dragged himself slowly, more and more slowly, along the snow.

But the Russians were beginning to come out of the oak-woods again. They climbed on the escarpment and down to the river once more. Now they were more careful than before; they didn't shout, and seemed timid. We began firing again. But this time they weren't coming to kill us; they only wanted to gather up the wounded who'd remained on the river. So I didn't fire any more, and shouted: 'Don't shoot. They're getting their wounded; don't shoot!'

The Russians seemed astounded at not hearing bullets coming at them any more; they stopped incredulously, got up on their feet, and looked around. I shouted: 'Don't shoot!' They hurriedly gathered up their comrades and loaded them on sledges, then ran along bent double, every now and again straightening up and looking towards us. They dragged them to the foot of the escarpment and then up towards their trenches. On the icy surface of the river the snow was all trampled. Their dead were also taken away, except for those under our wire.

Now everything was finally over. Over? Chizzarri came running towards me. 'Come, come to the Lieutenant quickly,' he said. 'He's bad, he wants you, come.' I could hear him sobbing as he ran along the trench in front of me. 'What is it? Is he wounded?' I shouted. 'No, hurry,' said Chizzarri. We went into the dugout of Pintossi's section; Lieutenant Moscioni was lying there on a straw mattress. By the light of the oil-lamp I could see he was pale and rigid, gritting his teeth. Over his uniform he wore his white overshirt. I knelt down beside him, took his hand and pressed it hard. He opened his eyes: 'I'm bad, Rigoni,' he said. He talked slowly, in a breath of a voice. I made him drink a little brandy that Chizzarri had. In the dugout three Alpini looked at us silently, squeezing the barrels of their rifles in clenched hands. 'I can't stand up,' he went on. 'Take over command of the strongpoint, be careful, as when the moon goes into the clouds the Russians will cross the river. Don't have me taken away, leave me here. Have I still got my pistol?' and he looked for the holster. I was bending over him and couldn't speak.

'Be careful. Is that you, Rigoni? The Russians are crossing the river. In case of retreat leave me here; I've still got my pistol. The Captain will give you the order; don't leave before it.' He was rigid and I went on squeezing his hand without speaking. Then I managed to say something to him. I got up. 'Take the stretcher and carry him away,' I said, turning to the Alpini. The Lieutenant didn't want this and shook his head. 'I've still got my pistol,' he said slowly. The Alpini didn't know who to obey. 'I'm in command here now; please go,' I say. And then to Chizzarri: 'Give him all the brandy there is, go with him and get his things, and return at once.' No one spoke any more. Chizzarri in a corner was rummaging in a pack and sobbing. The oil-lamp gave the dugout a snug look: on the props were nailed postcards with pictures of girls, flowers and villages in the mountains.

On the back of an old envelope I wrote and told the Captain what had happened to the Lieutenant and sent an Alpino to Company Headquarters: 'Tell him also that we urgently need ammunition'. 'Go, Rigoni,' the Lieutenant whispered, 'the Russians are crossing the river.'

I went outside again. Propped against the trench was a stretcher still marked with Marangoni's blood.

The news went round the strongpoint that the Lieutenant had gone. The section commanders came to me to ask: 'What shall we do now?' 'The same as you've done up to now,' I replied. 'Be calm, some other officer will come.' It never even entered my head to say: 'No one must move,' so sure I was that no one would go without an order. Minelli told me that Lombardi had been killed instantly by a bullet in the forehead while he was standing up shooting a machine-gun. I ordered him to be taken away to the kitchens, where the chaplain would look after him. Moreschi now pointed out that he had no more ammunition for the mortars. All was calm at Baffo's, over there they hadn't even seen the Russians coming to attack; and not fired a single shot. I had the machine-gun from there taken to Pintossi's sector which was the most exposed and so needed most ammunition. The heavy machine-gun was not functioning very well and Rosso, who was in charge of arms, had been kicked by the Lieutenant for not looking after it. I ordered it to be taken to bits and cleaned, then a burst or two fired, and a helmetful of coals put under it. But we had also run out of ammunition for it now.

'What's the matter with the Lieutenant?' the section commanders asked me. 'He's been overcome by cold, lack of sleep and exhaustion,' I replied. For days and days he's scarcely slept and never rested, he couldn't keep that up for long. 'Get some sleep,' I used to say to him. 'Rest; d'you see? It's all quiet now.' But he wouldn't. Either it was the weapons, or the positions, or the men, or a Russian patrol. He didn't want to. He fell from sheer exhaustion, like a mule. 'It was like being turned to ice,' he said to me later in Italy. 'I couldn't feel my legs any more, I couldn't feel anything. It was as if I'd only a head and very little of that. It was terrible.'

The Captain sent me down a note. He wrote that another officer would be coming to take over command of the strongpoint, and that he was sending me ammunition. We began firing again. The Russians were trying to cross the river at all costs. They were firing at us with mortars too, I noticed, when I heard a bang above my head; then something hit my helmet and snow and smoke entered my eyes. I didn't realize at once what had happened, then heard a cry for help nearby. One of Pintossi's section had his arm broken and the lower bit dangled down as if it were no longer part of his body. I twisted some string I had in my pocket tight round the wound to stop the blood that was pouring out. 'My arm! My arm!' he kept on saying, and screaming as he held his dangling arm with his other hand. 'You're lucky,' I said as I bound him up, 'it's not serious and you'll be home in a fortnight.' 'Really,' he said, 'I'll go home?' 'Yes, we might both of us have been killed. Now go back to the kitchens, I can't go with you; go back alone, we need everyone here. Quick; give me your cartridges,' and I emptied his pouches. He went off down the trenches moaning: 'My arm! My arm!' and trying to run in the dark.

Then I realized that a mortar-bomb had burst above our heads between us. His rifle lay broken on the ground. My hands were red with blood and my snow shirt dirty with blood and earth.

A little later silence fell again. But I felt no calm because a certain number of Russians had succeeded in infiltrating between us and Cenci. They were dangerous; they could get round us and penetrate the strongpoint from behind. With a machine-gun and a few men I moved farther back towards Cenci's. When I saw that on that side there were gaps in the barbed wire I was frightened and apprehensive. But the Russians were trying to penetrate in depth rather than come in our direction and we heard them firing towards the anti-tank ditch at the top of the valley leading to the rear areas. This time, I thought, they're going to wake up those lads in the rear areas. But the lads in the rear areas were left in peace for another day because our company recce section, led by Lieutenant Buogo, went to meet the Russians.

They were fine, the recce men were, all from the same village, Collio Val Trompia, and all related among themselves, or at least made love to each other's sisters. They had their own particular way of talking, always in shouts. That's how they went down to meet the Russians. After a burst of machine-gun fire we heard Buogo calling in the cold night air: 'Cenci! Cenci! Lieutenant Cenci!' And Cenci shouted back from his strongpoint: 'Buogo! Say, Buogo, what's the name of your girl?' And he repeated: 'What's the name of your girl?'

Buogo said a name. I and the Alpini round me began laughing. The name of a woman, of a fiancée, an Italian girl! Shouted out like that in the night while Russian machine-guns and Italian rifles were firing. 'Say, Buogo, what's the name of your girl? Buogo! Buogo! What's her name?' and the Alpini laughed. God! How pretty she probably was, and soft, and elegant. An officer's fiancée must be all that, and seemed so from her name. I imagined the two Lieutenants exchanging confidences and looking at photographs in their dugout. But to shout out her name in the night like that! I realized why Cenci wanted to know the girl's name. And all those who'd heard were laughing. Even the Russians must have understood. God! 'Let's drop everything here, there are so many pretty girls and such a lot of good wine, eh, Baroni? They've got their Katiuskas and Maruskas and vodka and sunflower seeds, and we our Marias and Teresas, wine and beech-woods.' I laughed, but the corners of my mouth were hurting and I was gripping the machine-gun.

There was firing down there among the thickets, and I heard clearly the voices of the recce men shouting that Lieutenant Buogo had been wounded in a leg and that they were carrying him back.

They were shouting in their jargon: 'Here they are! Come on! There are women too.' They might have been a company of a hundred strong and there were thirteen of them. They threw hand-grenades and shouted: 'We've got 'em, there are two women, come on!' They swore as they crashed about the thickets between us and Cenci.

Suddenly I noticed that dawn was beginning. A hare ran in front of me and went to hide among the dry grass on the bank. A runner came to warn me that a platoon of *Arditi* from the Morbegno strongpoint were coming to our help to wipe out the Russians who were still between us and Cenci. He told me that our recce men had just captured two Russian women who had gone into the attack in trousers and carrying sten-guns. Shortly afterwards I heard the *Arditi* of the Morbegno battalion. What lads these smugglers from Como were! They called out to each other, made noises, fired, swore. Almost like our own recce. 'At 'em! There! There!' they shouted and threw hand-grenades. The sun began rising behind the oak-woods. I'd seen it rising on so many mornings when our dug-outs and theirs were smoking away peacefully like the chimneys of a village in the Alps or the steppes; and everything had been calm and the virgin snow lay on the river, with no marks of blood or tracks of men on it.

I felt I couldn't keep my eyes open any longer. It was days since I'd washed and a crust of dirt had formed on my face. My hands were filthy with blood and earth, and smelly with smoke, and I longed for a morning like the others to be able to wash my face and go and sleep in my dugout. It was two nights and two days since I'd slept; and now there wasn't any ammunition, the Alpini were tired, the mail didn't arrive, the Lieutenant wasn't there. I was sleepy, hungry, and there were still so many things to do. But I had some cigarettes.

I sent a runner to tell the Captain that I urgently needed ammunition for all weapons, and lots of hand-grenades. I had the un-exploded cartridges, which jumped out when the machine-guns stuck, collected, to fire them from rifles.

The Alpini, tired, flung themselves down on the straw in the dug-out and snored with their rifles in their hands and their grenades in their pockets; sometimes one jumped to his feet shouting as he slept and immediately fell down again and snored. I left three sentries out, but couldn't sleep myself. The ammunition arrived. The drivers brought it down on their shoulders and hurried away as soon as they had put the cases down.

I was standing with a sentry looking at the bodies of the Russians which were still on the river and as I watched in the morning sun I noticed two Russians hiding very near us behind a mound on the river-bank. After I'd watched them a little they moved; one got to his feet and tried to run over to the other bank. I took aim. He might have been right in front of the barrel. I pulled the trigger and saw him fall flat on the snow. His other companion, who had got up to follow him, went back to hiding. I watched the fallen Russian through binoculars. He lay motionless. But why hadn't he waited till dark to pass over the other side? The sentry, who was watching him too, suddenly exclaimed: 'He's moving.' And I saw him jump up like a monkey and run towards the other bank. 'He's tricked me,' I shouted and laughed. But the sentry took the machine-gun from its position and fired it half standing up in the trench. I saw the Russian fall again, but not like before. He twisted about and dragged himself for a yard or two, and finally stopped with one arm stretched towards the river-bank, which was now near him. His companion who'd remained on our side tried to cross over again but a burst of machine-gun fire forced him to hide once more. I thought: 'He'll wait for night, now; it's worth his while.' I felt like shouting to him.

It was a fine sunny day; everything was clear and transparent, the only darkness was in men's hearts. Darkness like a stormy night on an ocean of pitch. Then I heard a great roar and felt the earth tremble under my feet. The snow fell into the trench, flames rent the sky above us and a high column of smoke went up from the other bank and hid the sun; it was yellow near the earth and blacker higher up. I saw my own terror reflected in the sentry's eyes, and moved about in the narrow trench. But my fear stopped me moving much or knowing what to do. I looked around and felt incapable of thought. The sentry was my mirror. Then I saw and heard the explosions going up behind Centi's strongpoint; lots of them, near each other and all at the same second. This, I managed to think, is the seventy-five shell Katiuska. God what a gun! It fired twice more and I held my breath each time. Finally our artillery began to reply. Then silence fell again.

I was waiting for the new officer to come and take over command of the strongpoint. I longed to sleep a bit, for an hour at least. Meanwhile time passed. It could have been nine, midday, two, I didn't know; the fifteenth or the sixteenth or the seventeenth of January.

I heard a voice shouting encouragement in Russian. I could understand a few words; country, Russia, Stalin, workers. At once I sent a sentry round the dugouts to get the men out with their weapons. They hurried out swearing, their eyes full of sleep, half shut in the sunlight. They smelt of smoke. I said: 'Don't fire before I give the order; keep ready.' Silence had returned. The voice the other side could no longer be heard. This side the complaints, the curses, the hurried steps, the noise of rifle-bolts had all stopped; we were all ready with our weapons set. Then the Russians rose to their feet on the edge of the woods and came out on to the escarpment. All was still calm. Not a rifle shot, not a cry. The silence amazed them. Perhaps they thought we'd already left. They sat down on the snow and slid down to the river-bank. But when the first of them reached the foot of the escarpment: 'Fire,' I shouted to the men at the machine-gun next to me. A short burst, then suddenly all our weapons began firing; the four light machine-guns, the heavy machine-gun, the thirty rifles, Moreschi's four mortars, and Baroni's two. All the bullets fell just where the escarpment joined the river-bank and as soon as the Russians put a foot on the bank, after sliding down on their bottoms, they were pinned down there. Those who had stayed on the edge of the wood and were standing up on the escarpment, hesitated and finally returned to the shelter of their trenches. The weapons stopped firing, but groans and wails for help came up from the river-bank. The most dogged tried to climb back up the slope to get into shelter again, and some succeeded. The voice I'd heard before started again. What was it saying? Perhaps calling for revenge for the comrades fallen in the snow or for the destroyed villages. Then they appeared again more purposefully. We began to fire once more. This time they didn't stop, or go back. Many fell under the escarpment, many. The others came on, shouting: 'Hurrah! Hurrah!' but few managed to get near our wire. I was firing my rifle at those who seemed most impetuous and were running ahead of the others. There were also some pretending to be dead; they lay motionless on the river and then when no one was watching got to their feet and began running towards us again. One used this trick three or four times until, when he'd got right under our trenches, he was really hit. He fell with his head and shoulders deep in the snow. One arm in the air continued to revolve more and more slowly until it stopped.

It must have been terrible to cross the river and run over the snow in full daylight, without the slightest shelter from the bullets and mortar-bombs hailing down. Only the Russians would dare that; but they couldn't reach us. They stopped trying and calm fell again. The snow on the river was redder and more churned, and those left lying on it more numerous too. I returned to the dugout, went up to the stove and looked at the fire, holding my rifle between my knees. The Alpini were talking of the attack they'd just repulsed.

'What've you got there, Sergeant-major?' Pintossi asked me. And he pointed to the place on my rifle where the bayonet was attached. I saw a machine-gun bullet buried in the wood there. 'You've had a lucky escape,' Pintossi said to me. I remembered then that during the attack I'd felt a hard jolt while I was kneeling in the trench and holding the rifle to my shoulder. The soldiers round the fire passed each other the rifle and observed: 'You've had a lucky escape; when you get home you must put up a little picture to the Madonna.' 'You might put up a couple.' 'If your number's not on it, you don't get it.' 'It's all fate . . .'

I took the bullet out and put it in the pocket of my jacket, saying: 'When I'm home I'll make my girl a ring from it.'

Finally Lieutenant Cenci came. I was pleased to see him, and as he came near I asked him: 'What's the name of your girl?' He laughed, then seeing me covered with blood, said: 'But, Rigoni, are you wounded?' 'No,' I said, 'it's not my blood.' He went on. 'A Russian might have called to me last night and what's why I asked Buogo what his girl's name was. A Russian couldn't know what it was. Buogo's had his leg broken by a bullet. Have you any cigarettes, Rigoni?' And he offered me one. We went round the trenches a bit then entered Pintossi's dugout. 'Not a single Russian's left on this side, Rigoni,' said Cenci (but I knew there was still one), 'and we've also captured two women. The drivers, grumbling, put them on sledges, then offered them cigarettes. "You should be cooking," they muttered to them, "and not fighting." Lieutenant Pendoli has come to my strongpoint. Try to rest and sleep now; you need it.'

I flung myself down on the boards; but I couldn't get to sleep. The grenades pressed on to my kidneys, the pouches full of cartridges weighed on my stomach. But even in a feather bed I wouldn't have been able to sleep. In an inner pocket of my jacket, in a wallet made from a piece of canvas, I kept my most precious letters, whose words seemed part of my being. Where was she now? Perhaps reading Latin poems in class or in her room; perhaps when looking among old books or sorting out old rubbish she's come across an Alpino star. But I'm silly to think about such things. Why doesn't sleep come? Why don't I sleep? Cenci was looking at me smiling. 'Why don't you sleep?' he said. 'What's your girl's name?' Luckily Tourn came to tell me that the rations had arrived and I went to Moreschi's dugout to get my share. There was an unusual confusion in there; blankets thrown about dirty on the floor, straw scattered among socks and handkerchiefs and pants. They were talking in whispers. Giuanin didn't say anything to me. He looked at me and in his eyes I could see all the things he wanted to say. Tourn didn't laugh any more and his black moustaches, usually so immaculate, were dirty with mucus. Meschini was busy with his pack. All the others were doing something. Two were out at the mortar post. Only Giuanin was doing nothing, sitting in his niche near the cold stove. 'Meschini,' I asked, 'why haven't you made polenta? I'm hungry; let's make it just once more.'

I ate my portion of the rations, but without enjoyment. A mortar-bomb or two exploded near our dugout and one above it. But our bunker was solid and well made; only a bit of earth trickled in and the windows broke.

The tinkle of the spoons in the mess-tins sounded stranger than the mortar-shells.

Before going out I said: 'Remember we must always stick together.'

I went back to Lieutenant Cenci and we set off towards one of the posts. We were alone. 'Tonight we must retreat,' said he. 'I've come here on purpose to tell you. Tonight we must retreat. Here, smoke. Take one. I'm going back to my strongpoint; perhaps Lieutenant Pendoli'll come here, perhaps you'll have to look after things yourself. The sections will leave the strongpoints one at a time. The first from here will stop half-way between your strongpoint and mine with their weapons at the ready, and wait for the second one before they start off again. So on till the last man's out. The rendezvous is at the kitchens at ——' and he told me a time I can't remember. 'The whole company will be waiting for you there. You must arrange the order of the sections.' I didn't reply; when the cigarette was finished I said: 'All right.'

I went back to the dugout to prepare my pack, changed into clean underclothes and left the dirty lice-ridden ones on the straw. I tried to put on as many clothes as I could wear without hampering my movements. The remaining two pairs of socks and jersey I threw into the pack together with some first aid kit, reserve rations, a tin of anti-freezing grease, and a blanket. I filled the rest of the pack with ammunition, mostly hand-grenades. Then with Tourn's help I tried to put it on my back, but perhaps it was too heavy. Next I burnt all the letters and postcards that I had, except for a small bundle. 'The Russians'll be curious to know what's written in them,' I thought. How it hurt to do all this. Then I shouted out loudly: 'Wear all the clothes you can get on without feeling too hampered. Put whatever you think most necessary into your packs and as much ammunition as you can. Lots of hand-grenades of the better types; the O.T.O.s and Bredas. Throw the S.R.C.M.s under the snow. No one must go on his own. We must all stick together the whole time. Remember that, always stick together.'

'When do we move?' they asked me. 'Tonight perhaps.' And I called Moreschi apart and said to him: 'Don't worry too much about the mortars, take them with you, but not with much ammunition. Hand-grenades and cartridges. It'll be all right.'

'Then, Sergeant-major,' shouted Meschini, 'we'd better make polenta just once more.' 'Yes, let's make it just once more,' I replied.

I went outside and repeated in the other dugouts what I'd said in mine. The men asked all sorts of questions and their eyes asked even more than their words. Around me was a great question mark.

Before nightfall Lieutenant Cenci went back to his strongpoint. 'I don't think they'll attack,' he said to me; 'now good luck, and don't let yourselves be taken by surprise. Till later, then——'

I felt all the responsibility weighing down on me. If a noise or anything else warned the Russians that we were about to leave the strongpoint, would we ever get home at all? The Alpini looked at me with tired sleepy eyes, waiting for me to say something. I tried to keep calm and thought of what I'd do if things went badly. When night fell I sent for all the section commanders; Minelli, Moreschi, Baffo, Rosso of the heavy and Pintossi. I asked: 'How's it going? Have you everything ready?' 'Nothing new to report,' they replied, 'all ready.' 'The first to leave,' I ordered, 'will be Moreschi's section. Apart from personal ammunition you must also carry the ammunition for the section weapons. Load up the men as much as possible; hide the remaining ammunition in the snow. We must load up like mules; we don't know what's ahead of us. If we can't carry the stuff any more we can leave it on the way. As soon as Moreschi reaches the ruined hut between us and Cenci, he'll wait with weapons at the ready for the second section to join them. Then he'll set off again. The second will wait for the third and so on. The second to leave will be Baffo's; then the heavy; then Minelli's; then

Pintossi's last.' I made them all repeat what they had to do. Then went on. 'If you hear firing don't worry; the section that's on the move will make for the kitchens; there the whole company will be waiting. The section commanders will leave last. Keep your men always near you and make sure your weapons are working. Don't leave spoons in the mess-tins, they make a noise and everything must be done in dead silence. It'll all be all right; keep on the alert, I'll send to tell you when you have to go. Off with you now, till later.'

Luckily it was a dark night. The darkest we'd had. The moon was behind clouds and it was very cold. The silence was heavy, like the night. Far away, beyond the clouds, behind us, one could see flashes of battle and hear a noise like wheels crunching over flints.

I stood outside the trench with a machine-gun under my arm and watched the darkness over towards the Russians. They were silent too; they might not have been there. 'Suppose they attack now?' I thought and shivered.

An Alpino whom I'd placed at the beginning of the trench leading to the valley came to tell me: 'Moreschi's section has passed. All's well.' 'Go and tell Baffo,' I said. I looked hard into the darkness, gripping the machine-gun, and trembled. 'Sergeant-major, Baffo's passed, all's well.' 'Go and warn the heavy.' 'The heavy's passed, all's well.' 'Talk quietly, go and tell Minelli.' Silence. I heard Minelli leaving, the steps getting farther away down the communication-trench, some whispered oaths. 'Sergeant-major, Minelli's passed too.' I looked ahead at the black river. I wasn't trembling any more. 'Get ready now.' I heard the sound of Pintossi's men getting ready, words being whispered, almost breathed, sounds of packs being loaded on to shoulders. 'Sergeant-major, can we go?' 'Go, Pintossi, go and don't make a row.' 'Are you coming?' 'Go, Pintossi, I'm coming.' The Alpino with the thick bristly beard came up to me. 'Aren't you coming?' he said. 'Go.' I was alone. I could hear the steps of the men growing fainter along the trench. The dugouts were empty. Although on the straw which had once been an *isba* roof lay dirty socks, empty cigarette packets, spoons, torn letters and on the props were nailed postcards of flowers, girls, babies, and mountain villages, the dugouts were empty, empty of everything and I was empty like them. I stood alone in the trench, looking at the dark night, thinking of nothing. I was clutching hard at the machine-gun. Then, pressing the trigger I fired off an entire belt; I fired off another and sobbed as I fired. Then I jumped down into the trench, and went to Pintossi's dugout to fetch my pack. There were some hand-grenades there and I threw them into the stove. I took both the safety catches out of some other grenades and set them down quietly at the bottom of the trench. Then I walked off towards the valley. It was beginning to snow. I was crying without knowing I was crying; my steps echoed alone in the dark trench. In my dugout, nailed to a prop, I'd left the crib in relief which my girl had sent me for Christmas.

II

The Bag

BEFORE reaching the anti-tank ditch I caught up with Pintossi's section. They were walking along bent and silent. Every now and again one of them let out a curse just to express the desperation weighing on him. Where were we going now? Would the Russians notice we'd evacuated the strongpoint? And follow us at once? Would we be made prisoner? I stopped to listen and looked back. All was black and silent.

At the anti-tank ditch some Alpini of the 113 mm. support guns were putting down mines. 'Quick,' they said to us. 'You're the last. We must destroy the bridge.'

When I'd passed the bridge and was on the other side I felt as if I were in a different world. Never, I realized, would I return to that village on the Don; I knew I was leaving Russia and the land of 'that village' for ever. Now it'll have been rebuilt, the sunflowers will be blooming again in the gardens round the *isbas* and the old man with a white beard like Uncle Jeroska fishing in the river once more. When we had dug out the communication-trenches we'd found potatoes and green vegetables in the snow and earth; now they will have levelled it all and in their spring digging found empty cartridge cases from Italian weapons. The children will be playing with them, and I'd like to say to them: 'Look, I was here too, by day I slept under there, and by night I went round your gardens which didn't exist then any more. Have you found the anchor?'

At a certain point I was supposed to meet the rest of the company who were waiting for me; I found them farther back, at the kitchens. When the Captain heard me arriving, he came towards me swearing and kicking up the snow with anger, thrust his watch under my nose and said: 'Look, you fool, we're more than an hour late. We're the last. Couldn't you get here before?' I tried to say something in explanation, but he told me to shut up. 'Go ahead with your platoon,' he said.

I found my machine-gun platoon. They were pleased to see me, but all of them weren't there. Lieutenant Sarpi wasn't with us any more; one or two others were in hospital wounded. Antonelli came up to me: 'It's the end this time,' he said, 'it's all up.' We started walking down the road we'd come along early in December when we were relieving the Valcismon della Julia Division. A 75/13 mm. fired a round or two. We walked along with our heads low, one behind the other, mute as shadows. It was cold, very cold, but we were sweating under the weight of our packs full of ammunition. Every now and again someone fell into the snow and got up with difficulty. The wind rose. First it was almost imperceptible, then it got stronger until it became a torture. It was blowing, immense and free, off the limitless steppes. In the cold darkness it found us, poor creatures lost in the war, knocked us about, made us stagger. We had to hang on tight to the blankets protecting our heads and shoulders. But the snow got in underneath them and pricked our faces, collars, wrists, like pine needles. We walked one behind the other, our heads down. Although we were sweating under our blankets and snow shirts, if we stopped for a second we shivered with cold. And it was very cold. The pack full of ammunition got heavier at every step; it seemed to be going to break off at any moment, like a young oak branch loaded with snow. 'Now I'll throw myself down on the ground and never get up again, it's all over. Another hundred yards and I throw away my ammunition. Isn't this night and this torture ever going to end?' But we walked on. One step after the other, one step after the other. I felt as if I was going to fall face downwards into the snow and suffocate, with two knives stuck under my armpits. When will it end? Alps, Albania, Russia. How many miles? How much snow? Sleepiness? Thirst? Has it always been like this? Will it always be like this? I shut my eyes but went walking on. One step. Another step. The Captain who was leading the company lost touch with the other units. We were off our right road. Every now and again he lit his torch under his blanket and consulted his compass. One or two soldiers slowly detached themselves from their sections, sat down on the snow and began loosening their packs. There was nothing I could say, except: 'Hide it under the snow, keep the hand-grenades.' Antonelli was carrying the barrel of the heavy machine-gun; he wasn't swearing any more, not because he didn't want to, but because he couldn't. In the dark I found myself stepping on some mysterious solid objects; cases of 45 mm. mortar-bombs. They came from Moreschi's section. I went up to him and said: 'You and your section must help the others to carry the heavy machine-gun and the ammunition for it. Leave the mortars,' I added more quietly, 'and the other cases; try to do it so that the Captain doesn't notice.' Ahead they'd stopped, and we all stopped. No one spoke, it was like a column of ghosts. I flung myself down on the snow with my blanket over my head, opened my pack and buried two packets of machine-gun cartridges in the snow. We began walking again, after a bit I got Antonelli to pass me the heavy machine-gun and handed him over the two spare barrels I'd been carrying up till then. Antonelli opened his mouth, took a deep breath and swore everything that came into his head. He seemed to have become so light that the wind would carry him away; and I to be sinking under the weight: 'Come on,' I said, 'we must stick together.' Where were we walking that night? On a comet or an ocean? Something infinite, anyway.

Sprawling on the snow against a bank on the other side of the track was a runner from Company Headquarters. He'd let himself fall on the snow, and looked at us as we passed. He said nothing. We felt his despair too. A long time after, in Italy (and there was sun, a lake, green trees, wine, girls walking up and down), the father of this lad came to ask from the few of us who had survived, news of his son. No one could tell him anything. He looked at us angrily: 'Tell me something, even if he's dead, tell me everything you can remember, anything at all.' He talked in jerks, gesticulating; he was decently dressed, being the father of an Alpino. 'The truth's hard,' I said then, 'but as you want to hear it I'll tell you what I know.'

He listened to me without speaking, without asking me anything. 'There,' I ended, 'that's how it was.' He took me by the arm and led me to a tavern. 'A litre of wine and a couple of glasses . . . Another litre.'

I looked at the portrait of Mussolini hanging on the wall and clenched my teeth and fists. The old man didn't talk and he didn't cry . . . Finally he shook my hand and went back to his village.

That night was endless. We were supposed to reach a place in the rear areas where there were stores and headquarters. But we didn't know any names of places in the rear. The telephonists, the typists and the other base troops knew all the names. We didn't even know the name of the village where our strongpoint had been; and that's why here you'll find only the names of soldiers and objects. All we knew was that the river in front of our strongpoint was the Don, and that we were any number of miles, a thousand to ten thousand, from home. And where east and west were. Nothing more.

We were supposed to reach a village where, the officers said, we could rest and eat. But where was it? In some other world? Finally, far away, a faint light could be seen; it grew and grew until it lit up the sky with a rosy glow. But was this red light in the sky or on the earth? Then as we got nearer we made out that it was a burning village. But the torture didn't let up and there was always that sensation of daggers sticking under the armpits, and we were breaking under the weight of the packs and weapons. Now other red lights could be seen in the dark. The snow pricked at our eyes but we walked on. We reached a village, made out the shapes of *isbas* and heard dogs barking; a road could be felt under the snow. But we couldn't stop, we had to go on walking still. There were others walking near there too. Russians perhaps. But it's better to die. One of them comes up to me, pulls my blanket, and looks at me fixedly: 'What unit are you from?' he asks me. '55th Vestone, 6th Alpini,' I reply. 'D'you know Sergeant-major Rigoni?' says the shadow. 'Yes,' I reply. 'Is he alive?' he asks. 'Yes,' I say, 'he's alive. But who are you?' 'I'm a cousin of his,' he says. 'But where is he?' 'I'm Rigoni,' I say, 'but who are you?' 'Adriano.' And he takes me by the shoulders and calls me by my name and shakes me. 'How are things, cousin?' says Adriano. But I can't manage to say a word. Adriano brings his eyes close up to my face and says: 'How are things, cousin?' 'Bad,' I say, 'things are bad. I'm sleepy, I'm hungry, I can't take any more. Things are just about as bad as they could be.' Adriano, he told me later at home, was astounded to hear me talk in this way that night. 'When I'd met him he'd always been calm and jolly,' he said at home, 'but that night. That night!'

Adriano took a tin of jam and a two-kilo piece of Parmesan cheese out of his pack. 'I got this stuff from a store dump,' he said, 'eat up.' I tried to break off a piece of the cheese with my bayonet so as to hand him back the rest. But when I took my gloves off I felt an

agonizing pain in my hands and couldn't cut with them. My hands
were not following my brain and I looked at them as if they weren't
mine and felt like weeping for these poor hands that didn't want to
belong to me any more. I began banging them hard against each
other, on my knees, on the snow; and I couldn't feel either the flesh
or the bone; they were like bits of tree-bark, like shoe-soles; eventually I felt as if they were being pierced by lots of needles, and little
by little these hands with which I'm now writing became mine
again. How many things my body can remind me of.

We started walking on again into the night. 'What about the
others from home, Adriano?' I asked. 'They're all well,' he replied.
'But I must go back to my unit, we'll see each other again.
Keep going, cousin.' 'We'll be seeing each other,' I said, 'keep
going.'

On, on, we must stick together. I can't make the effort to talk to
the others about home or wine or spring-time. What's the use?
Oh, to fling oneself on the snow and sleep and dream of such things
and then vanish into nothing, into emptiness, and lose oneself, melt
into the earth with the snow in spring. It was all dark, and far away
in the sky, were red reflections of burning villages. Another step, yet
another; the snow pierced the blanket and pricked my face, throat
and wrists. The wind took my breath away and tried to snatch off
the blanket. I ate a little of the cheese Adriano had given me. It was
difficult to break with my teeth, and then it was like chewing sand;
and I felt that with each mouthful I was swallowing blood from my
gums and lips. The breath froze on my beard and moustache and
formed icicles with the snow carried by the wind. I pulled these
icicles up with my tongue and sucked them. Dawn came. And the
torture increased. And the cold increased. But now I ask myself;
if we hadn't been through this hell would we have escaped from the
Russians?

That night Lieutenant Cenci and his platoon were acting as rear-
guard. At a certain point they had stopped at an *isba* to rest, but if
two women hadn't woken them in time for them to start walking
hurriedly on they'd have been surprised by Russians who were
already near their *isba*. The dawn was grey and the sun never came
out and there was only snow and the wind and we in the snow and
the wind. No one wanted to carry the heavy machine-gun and its

cases of ammunition any more; and when someone hoisted one of these up over his pack no one would take it over from him. I tried to convince the others that we must keep the things with us. The Bredas in my section were the best weapons in the company and I knew what it meant for riflemen to have a heavy machine-gun with them during an attack. We must take it with us at any sacrifice. But when that morning, after that night, I had to hoist the tripod and a case of ammunition up over my pack, the daggers striking under my armpits seemed to be reaching my heart, and my lungs were left without air. Whenever one took any of these things off a comrade, he seemed almost airborne; he would sigh, breathe deep, swear and then say a Hail Mary to himself.

We were walking along a road and the snow was heaped up at the sides; but it was old snow, not like the fresh stuff torturing us. On the right was a row of *isbas*. We were going along in groups now with straggling ends, it was difficult to keep the platoon together. The wind whistled freely and agonizingly between the groups. All was grey and we could see little.

Here there must have been stores dumps at one time, for there were wisps of straw in the snow. Think of it; straw where there were once piles of grain. There were also some cases of hard biscuits. As soon as they see these the Alpini rush towards them; though they turn out to be empty, there must still be something in the bottoms for the men jostle and push for room to plunge their hands in. Those beneath shout out. Then slowly they all go off. One of them still stays by the cases, turning them over and grubbing about in the snow.

The Captain, who's ahead of us all, stops and looks at his compass. But where are we? At one side of the road I see a dark motionless mass. A lorry? or a cart? or a tank? It's a broken-down abandoned car.

A sense of apprehension comes over me and I feel that Russian tanks are about to come at us out of the snow. 'On,' says the Captain, 'keep at it, we must hurry. On.' Finally we reach a big village where there'd been headquarters and stores. The agony stops, but everything is grey; the snow, the *isbas*, us, the mules, the sky, the smoke coming out of the chimneys, the mules' eyes and ours. They're all the same colour. And my eyes won't keep open any longer, my throat feels as if it's full of stones jumping about inside it. We're legless, headless, armless, just exhaustion and sleepiness, and throats full of stones.

We see the Major commanding the battalion come out of an *isba*. 'Go into the *isbas* in the warmth and rest,' he says. 'The other companies have been here some hours already. Where've you been? How you must have wandered last night! Go into the *isbas*,' says the Major. Perhaps he thinks he's talking to ghosts, because we stand there steaming like mules. 'Go into the warmth and rest,' says the Captain, 'we leave again in a few hours. Arrange the platoons in the *isbas*,' he says to the officers and to me, 'and get them to clean their weapons.'

When we'd left the strongpoint the section had been complete; looking at them now, I realize that a number of men are missing; perhaps they've got dispersed in the snow, or stopped at some *isba*, or gone into cover as soon as they'd arrived here. But no one bothers to check who's missing. Those who remain go off in groups to look for an empty *isba* to get into. I stay outside alone and wander along one road after the other without knowing where to go. Why haven't I gone with my comrades of the platoon? With ¬y own men? I don't know. There I am alone, out in the snow; and I don't know where to go. Finally I knock at a door or two. But either they don't reply or they won't open up. Most of the houses are occupied by men in the transport, supply, stores or medical units. I want to sleep a bit in the warmth, why don't you let me in? Aren't I a man like you? No, I'm not like you; I'm all alone looking round in the middle of the road. An old man comes up and points behind a row of *isbas* to a garden with a heap of earth in it. A roof is sticking out of the earth, with smoke coming from it. He signs to me to go down there. It's an anti-aircraft shelter. At ground level are two little windows with glass in them. I go down a stair cut out of the earth and knock at the door. Someone comes to open it, an Italian soldier. 'There are three of us here already,' he says. 'And a Russian family.' And he shuts the door again. I knock. 'Let me in,' I say, 'I won't stay long. I only want to sleep a bit, I won't stay long.' But the door stays shut. I knock, the door opens again, a Russian woman appears and signs to me to enter. It's hot in here, it's like my dugout at the strongpoint, except that here there's a Russian woman with three

children and three Italian deserters. But now only one of these is
here because the other two are out. The remaining one looks at
me askance. The woman helps me to take my greatcoat off. My face
must be in a real state, for she gazes at me with eyes so full of pity
that they're almost weeping. But I can't feel anything now. The
deserter looks at me from a corner, and when he sees that I've two
stripes on my sleeves and some above my pocket, tries to start a con-
versation. God, the army! Supposing I'd been an ordinary driver?
Or rifleman? Or mule? Or ant? I don't reply to his questions and
take off my helmet and balaclava. It makes me feel quite naked.
Then I empty out the grenades from my pockets and put them in
my helmet, and take off the pouches which are weighing on my
belly. I take a handful of coffee mixed with snow from a pocket and
grind it in the top of my mess-tin with my bayonet handle. The
woman laughs, the deserter sits quiet, looking at me. The woman
puts water on to boil and makes two boys get up who are sprawling
on pillows looking at me. She takes the pillows and puts them on a
sort of platform, on which she also throws a blanket; mine she
hangs up to dry by the fire. Then she signs to me to get up on the
platform and sleep. I sit down with my legs dangling over and
finally say: '*Spaziba.*' The woman and even the children smile at
me. The deserter is still looking silently at me. I take the jam
Adriano gave me, it's all I have, and eat it; I try to offer it to the
children but the woman won't let me: '*Cusciai,*' she says, '*cusciai,*'
in a whisper, smiling. When the water boils she makes coffee for me,
and so finally, after all this time, I get something warm inside me.
I arrange my place for sleeping, and put the rifle and helmet with
the grenades down beside me. 'This morning the Russian tanks
were here,' says the deserter. 'But what are you doing?' I ask him,
'what are you waiting for? Aren't you going with your unit?' He
doesn't reply. Outside it's cold, there's the steppes, the wind, the
snow, emptiness all round, the Russian tanks, and here he's warm
with his two companions and the Russian woman. 'Wake me if you
hear firing,' I say. On a bracket, against the yellow earth walls, is an
old alarm clock, and I make signs for the woman to wake me when
the little hand has reached the number two. That's the time I must
be back with the company. It's eleven now, I'll get three hours'
sleep. And I fling myself down on the pillows, fully dressed and

with my boots on. But why can't I sleep? Why do I keep on thinking of my men, who are warm in the *isbas*? Why do I keep my ears cocked for the sound of firing? Why doesn't sleep come? It's so many days since I slept. The two deserters who were out return and I hear them talking among themselves; then a baby cries; I lie there with my eyes open looking at the yellow earth walls. Strongpoint, miles, comrades, Russians, corpses on the river, Katiuska, friends from home, Lieutenant Moscioni, hand-grenades, Russian woman, mules, bugs, rifle. Does green grass still exist? Does green exist? And then I sleep, sleep, sleep. Without dreaming of anything. Like a stone under water.

It's late when the Russian woman wakes me, she's let me sleep half an hour over time. Hurriedly I tie my blanket to my pack, put the grenades back in my pockets and the helmet on my head. When I'm ready to leave the woman hands me a cup of hot milk. Milk like one drinks in the mountains in summer; or has with polenta on January evenings. Not hard tack and tinned food, not frozen soup, not iced bread, not wine glassy with cold. Milk. And I'm no longer in the war in Russia, but among cows smelling of milk in meadows flowering among oak-woods, or in warm kitchens on January evenings when women knit and old men smoke their pipes and tell stories. The cup of milk steams in my hands, the vapour goes up my nose and into my blood. I drink. Then I hand the empty cup back to the woman, saying: '*Spaziba.*'

After that I turn to the three deserters: 'Aren't you coming?' 'But where d'you think you're going?' one of them replies; 'we're surrounded by Russians and here we're warm.' 'So I see,' I say. 'I'm off. Good luck to you.' And I'm outside again.

The whole village was buzzing as if a stick had been put into an ant heap in the woods. Boys, women, children, old men were going into the *isbas* with faggots and bundles and coming out at once with empty sacks under their arms. They were going to the burning stores dumps and taking everything they could save from the flames. Amid the mob were sledges, mules, lorries, cars coming and going aimlessly up and down the roads; a group of German tanks soon opened a passage for itself. Yellow, acrid smoke hung over the village and wrapped the houses. The sky was grey, the *isbas* grey, the trampled snow was grey. I still had the flavour of milk in my mouth, but now I was outside. Now I was walking towards home, whatever happened.

My hands in my pockets, I looked at what was going on round me, feeling alone. Passing in front of a building, the school perhaps, I saw two flags hanging down over the road; one was Italian and the other of the Red Cross, the last so big it nearly touched the ground. Suddenly I felt sad. I imagined the empty village with the fires dying down in the stores dumps, the inhabitants shut in the *isbas*, an abandoned mule or so rooting among the cabbage stalks which showed above the snow. I imagined the Russian soldiers arriving. The mules scarcely moving their ears as the tanks ground by, our wounded looking out of the hospital windows, then everything grey and the two flags hanging down over the deserted road.

Now the walking wounded were coming out of the hospital and trying to get lifts on passing sledges and trucks.

I couldn't see a single soldier from my company or battalion. Perhaps they had already left. I saw a man from the Cervino Battalion walking alone like me. I called him and we went along together. We exchanged news of acquaintances. I'd taken part in an action with the Cervino the winter before. 'And Sergeant Chienale?' I asked. 'Dead.' 'And Lieutenant Sacchi!' 'Dead.' And many others were dead too. A handful, ten perhaps, were left of the Cervino, which had been more dashing than a Bersaglieri battalion.

I crossed the village and passed near the burning supply dumps. Later I heard that Alpini arriving from the front had gone among the abandoned dumps; and the supply men had said to them: 'Take what you like.' They found chocolate, brandy, wine, jam, cheese. They fired into the barrels of brandy and put their mess-tins underneath. After all they'd been through, they were finally drinking and eating and sleeping again. Many of them never woke up; they were burnt or frozen to death. Others woke to find the barrels of Russian guns in their faces. But one or two managed to get away and tell the tale.

Just before leaving the village, I managed to catch sight in the confusion of some men from my company. I joined them. At the passage of a wide ditch, before the open steppes, was a great mass of trucks, sledges, and cars. Lorries were lying overturned at the bottom of the ditch and curses and shouts came up, calls for help,

for a push or to clear the way. I enjoyed seeing the overturned
lorries which couldn't move, and remembered how, the previous
summer, the long columns of transport used to pass us and the
chocolate-coloured dust stuck to our sweating bodies as we walked
along under our packs, penetrating into our throats, making us spit
yellow for weeks.

And the men of the rear supply and depot units had watched us
passing from the sides of the truck and laughed. Yes, the swine,
they'd laughed. 'But this time it's they who have to get a move on.
Like hell they'll have to get a move on. If they want to reach home
they'll have to get a move on!' That's what I was thinking as I
watched them toiling round their vehicles which were full of loot or
officers' baggage or some stuff like that. Behind them the flames
and smoke from the fires were rising and the sound of gunfire getting nearer. 'Now, you shirkers, the time's come for you too to
leave the girls in the *isbas*, the typewriters and all the rest. Learn to
fire a rifle, come with us if you want to; as for us, we're through.'

I was thinking that, and the thought gave me energy and made me
kick up the snow beside the track. I walked along more quickly and
went ahead. We climbed up the other side of the ditch. The column
was winding away through the steppes then vanishing behind a
distant rise, making a black S-shaped coil on the snow. It seemed
impossible there could be so many of our men, so long a column in
Russia. How many strongpoints like ours had there been? That long
column was to stay in my eyes for days and the memory of it in my
head for ever.

But it was going along very slowly, too slowly, and I left the track
to try and get farther ahead. We still had two Bredas with a thousand
rounds or so and our reserve rations. The weight made us sink into
the snow, but we still went much faster than the column. The straps
of the packs sawed at our shoulder blades. Antonelli was swearing
as always and every now and again Tourn looked at me as if to say:
'We'll make it, won't we?' With us we had a man from Moreschi's
section who was trying to lag a pace or two behind so as to avoid
his turn at carrying the guns. Antonelli cursed him with the finest
slang from the Veronese slums. Every now and again we ran into
some man lying supine and dazed in the snow, watching us pass
without making any sign. At the side of the track an Italian officer

in riding boots and spurs was waving his arms about and shouting nonsense. He was drunk and swayed about, fell on the snow, got up shouting something or other and then fell down again. With him was a Carabiniere trying to hold him up and pull him forward. Finally they stopped behind an isolated straw shack. Farther on I met others from my company, then four men of my platoon, among them Turrini and Bosio. They had rigged up a little sledge and loaded the heavy machine-gun and three cases of ammunition on it. From various parts of the column I'd succeeded in collecting nearly all my platoon together. Every now and again I was pleased to see another group joining ours, which was quite big by now; they called each other by name and joked and laughed about our state. Those who were walking along in the column raised their eyes from the snow, gave us a glance, then lowered their heads. 'We're together again,' I said. 'Let's walk on quickly.'

Night came and we reached a little village in the steppes. I didn't know what day or night it was, I knew it was very cold, and that we were hungry too. We joined up with the other platoons of the company and battalion. Now we were among our own people again; we could hear Brescian dialect being spoken around. *Corai s'cec, forza s'cec, forza s'cec.* Major Bracchi was talking Brescian too, with cap on head, Vibram boots, cigarette in mouth, rank badges on the sleeves of his greatcoat, firm walk, blue eyes and voice that spread calm. 'Bear up, lads,' he was saying. 'We'll be home eating kid's meat for Easter.' He called one or other of us by name and smiled.

'Goat-beard,' he said to me (that's what he called me, 'goat-beard' or 'old man'), 'you seem to've got rather thin and run down. A plate of spaghetti and a litre of red wine is what you need.' 'God if I don't!' said I, 'even two. Don't you?' 'Sir,' Bodei said to him, 'you should be confined to barracks, a button's missing on your greatcoat and your feather is askew.' 'F—— you,' replied the Major. When he was speaking to us the Major smiled and joked, then he'd become serious and his eyes go dim. And I thought: 'Easter is still a long way off, we've only just passed Christmas; and there are thousands of miles in front of us.'

It was night and very cold, and we were standing there in the snow waiting for orders. I saw that the Captain was so tired he couldn't stand much more. Lieutenant Cenci, wrapped in a blanket like a shawl, was smoking one cigarette after the other and cursing every now and again. When he drew in the smoke I could see the end light up like a cat's eye. He was talking a bit to a man in his platoon and swearing gently in his harmonious drawing-room voice. He came up to me: 'How goes it, old man?' he said. 'All right,' I replied, 'all right; but it's a bit cold.' God, it was cold!

There was confusion all round us; we could hear German, Hungarian, and every dialect of Italian being spoken. Some *isbas* and supplies were burning nearby, and the snow round them reflected the red glow up to the village boundaries where the steppes began. And burning also behind us was the village we'd left that afternoon. Every now and again explosions and the sound of engines could be heard, but it seemed as if there was nothing any more beyond the red of the fires. The world ended there. God! and we had to go out beyond into that darkness. Our boots were like wood, the dry snow like sand and the stars seemed to tear at our skins like spurs. Not a soul was left in the village; not even any cows, pigs or geese. Far away in the dark, dogs could be heard barking. Our mules were still with us, dreaming, their ears drooping, of Alpine paths and tender grass. Steam poured from their nostrils like whales; their coats were covered with white frost and had never been so glistening. And there were lice too; our own lice which didn't care a damn about anything, as they were snug and warm in the most hidden places. Now, I thought, if I were to die what would happen to the lice on me? When the blood in my veins was like red glass would they die later than me, or would they hold out till spring? When at the strongpoint we used to spread out our vests in forty-six degrees of frost for two days and two nights, as soon as we put them on after drying them near the stove the lice showed up at once. They were strong and healthy.

'Rigoni, d'you want a cigarette?' says Cenci. I smoke, at least the smoke's warm. Antonelli grunts: 'Are we moving on or not? What are we doing here?' And curses.

Some men who were here before us tell us that Russian tanks had already reached this place once, bringing terror with them. But now we're in strength; a Hungarian division, a German armoured unit, the Vicenza Division, what remains of the Julia, the Cuneense and we of the Tridentina. And then all the service units; transport, supplies, engineers, sanitary troops, etc. A good number of the latter are sure they're already prisoners and have thrown their weapons away in the snow. We're prisoners, I think and say, only when a Russian soldier can make us walk wherever he wants by pointing a gun at us, but not now.

'Sergeant-major, shall we ever get home?' Giuanin comes up. 'Yes, we'll see each other there again, Giuanin,' I say. 'But don't think of home now, think of jumping up and down on the snow so's to prevent your feet from freezing.' Major Bracchi, who'd gone off to get orders, returns. Finally we begin moving, but in reverse. 'We're going as rear-guard,' says Lieutenant Pendoli. 'It's always us who get the dirty jobs,' we grumble. (And the Tirano men will say the same.) 'Vestu! Come on this way,' shouts Bracchi.

The snow's so deep that we either knock our helmets against the man in front or fall in and have to flounder hurriedly on to keep up. The stores and the *isbas* are burning and here and there we hear shouts in German. We pass near some big Panzers with their engines running (so as not to freeze up, I think). As I walk along like this in the snow my boot kicks into a tin and I take it up. It's half-full and by the light of the fires I see it contains food. I put in my hand without taking off my glove; it's like Moses' manna; jam and butter mixed together. I lick my glove and moustache, and eat walking along, sharing it with those near me.

I don't know how long we walked; every step seemed a mile and every second an hour; it was endless. Finally we stopped at some isolated *isbas*. I arranged my platoon in a walled building; it must have been the school or the village hall. We also found some transport drivers there. They're like lice, get in everywhere. Finally we've a fire and warmth and even straw on the floor. Ah! How lovely it is to fling ourselves down and take off our helmets and put our packs under our heads, all lying close up near the fire. Finally we can shut our eyes and sleep.

But who's calling me outside? Go to the devil, let me sleep. Someone opens the door and calls my name: 'Report to the Captain, he wants you.' I feel a burning inside me. I get up, my companions are already asleep and snoring. To get out I have to stumble over their feet, they swear, open their eyes, turn over on the other side and go to sleep again. It's cold outside; all is silent, the runner has disappeared, instead there are as many stars as in a September sky. But they were lovely then, the September nights among the wheat fields and butterflies; the stars were warm and loving, like the earth. Now I don't know if I'm in a nightmare or if a malignant spirit is amusing himself behind my back. There's no one outside and I go to look for the Captain. What does he want to say to me? I look in one *isba* and don't find him, knock at others. They reply in German: '*Raus!*' or in Brescian: '*Inculet!*' I find some riflemen in my company and they ask if I'd like to come in and sleep with them. 'I'm looking for the Captain,' I say. 'Is he here?' 'No,' they reply. I go round among the Hungarians' horses and look for him; I call him along the tracks that lead to the steppes. No one replies. The stars are tearing at my flesh, I feel like crying and cursing. I'd like to kill someone on the spot. I stamp at the snow, wave my arms, grit my teeth; the stones jump about in my throat. Calm yourself! Don't go mad! Calm! Go back to your platoon in the *isba*, go to sleep again. Who knows what tomorrow will bring? Tomorrow! But it's already dawn, over there day is beginning to break. The mornings at the strongpoint when I'd return to the dugout and find coffee hot and ready; the mornings before I became a soldier when I used to go and gather wood and heard the wild cockerels singing! the mornings when I went up to mountain huts on my grey mule. And she'll be sleeping between clean sheets in her city by the sea, and the first light of dawn will be entering the room. Why not fling myself down on that heap of snow and sleep, how soft it must be! Be careful, be careful now, go and find the *isba* your platoon is in. I clench my teeth and fists and kick the snow. I find the *isba* again, go in and drop down among the warm bodies of my comrades. But I scarcely get an hour's sleep before Cenci bangs on the door and shouts: 'Machine-gun platoon, wake up! Be quick, we're leaving. Wake up, Rigoni!' And I hear my companions getting silently up and wrapping their blankets and then Antonelli swearing. How I'd like to sleep, to sleep just a little still, only a little; I can't stand it any more; I'll either go mad or shoot myself. Yet I get up, go out, call the platoon together, see who's missing, go and look for late-comers, and as I do this become myself again. I no longer think of either sleep or cold. I make sure we've not left anything in the *isba*, ammunition or arms, inspect those present, see if their weapons are clean, pull the bolts and press the triggers. This body of mine is really amazing; muscles, nerves, bones; I never thought before they could endure so much. We go towards the far end of the village. The other platoons of the company have already left and we are the last. We pass the sledges of the Hungarians and a group of Alpini artillery. At the bottom of a shallow ditch we meet up with the rest of the company. But the Captain's not there. Major Bracchi is walking impatiently up and down the snow. He calls me and sends me to look for the Captain and a company that's missing. 'Be quick,' says Bracchi, 'we must go into attack and try to open a way out of the bag.' I retrace my steps; and find the Captain. He's sitting on a sledge and calls me while I'm still some way off. 'Rigoni, friend,' he says, 'I've got fever. I wanted to stop in an *isba*; no, I'm not well. Where's the company?' 'Captain,' I say, 'the company's down there,' and I point. 'They're waiting for you, the Major has sent me to look for you.'

The Captain is with his batman and the sledge-driver. He doesn't look jovial and lively any more; with his blanket drawn up over his head like a shawl and his snowshirt pulled up to his collar, he no longer looks like a smuggler of Valstagna.

'Take me where the company is,' says the Captain, 'don't leave me alone. I'm your Captain, aren't I? You're not going to leave me alone when I'm your Captain! I've got fever,' he repeats. 'Let's go,' I reply.

I find a Lieutenant from the missing company, with his platoon. 'The company's coming,' he says. But meanwhile it's getting late and our place has been taken by the Verona and a battalion of the 5th. One can already hear firing. Heavy firing. We can hear the sharp bursts of the Russian machine-guns, and our heavies, some mortars and even hand-grenades exploding. It must be tough up there. I feel a quiver all over my body, as if the bullets were cutting right into me; every now and again I hold my breath. And I feel a great gloom and a great longing to cry. It's up there they're firing; at a row of *isbas* on the back of a rise. And we must pass, they say, because beyond it there's a road by which the German motorized troops can reach us.

But the Russians don't want to let us pass. They fire, fire, fire, and I feel frightened, as I wouldn't if I were with them. Something

seems to break away from me at every burst, at every explosion.
Here we're ready to start and I long to stop waiting about in this
cold ditch behind the village, and to end this agony. Will they pass
or is it really all up? My companions are tired, every now and again
a man from my platoon goes off and wanders around the village
among the Hungarian sledges. The latter are the most passive and
neutral of all. Their sledges are loaded down with lard, sausages,
sugar, vitamin tablets, but no arms or ammunition. The Alpini
soldiers wander round their sledges, looking idle and aimless, with
their hands in their pockets. When they return to us they pull pieces
of lard and sausage from under their overcoats. We've lit a big fire,
and stand round it in a circle, turning every now and again to warm
ourselves on both sides. We talk; our principal subject of conversa-
tion is wine. 'When I get home I want to bathe in a vat of wine,' says
Antonelli. 'And I to eat three whole mess-tins full of spaghetti,'
adds Bodei (he'd even forgotten that at home one eats out of a
plate), 'and smoke a cigar as long as an alpenstock.' Looking at the
fire, Meschini says, in a serious tone of conviction; 'And I to get
drunk on grappa and melt all the snow in Russia with my breath.'
But every now and again we're silent and listen to the firing up
there. 'They're still firing,' says Antonelli, and curses. 'Tourn!' he
shouts, clapping him on the back: 'A litre and a half of Barbera and
Grignolino!' And Tourn raises his head, his squirrel eyes light up
under his balaclava: 'Any drink,' he says. But there there's nothing
except a fire that smothers you in front and snow that freezes you
behind. Lieutenants Cenci and Pendoli call the roll near the company sledges; there's something to distribute. They are the last
rations; the last the cooks have managed to carry as far as this. I
was sure there was nothing left. The bread sacks are encrusted with
snow and smell of onions, meat, jam, coffee; the cooks smell of it
too. There are two rolls each, hard, old and frozen; Parmesan cheese
also comes out of the sledges, and this is frozen too. Lieutenant
Cenci had to take a hatchet to break it up and then I help him with
a bayonet to portion out the rations for the platoon. There's also
brandy. We smell it when the cooks draw out the barrels, and sniff
the air like hunting dogs; those who were some way off hurry near.
'Section commanders out with your mess-tins!' How often in four
years of service I've portioned out the rations; a mess-tin filled up

to the nails on the handle equals eight rations of wine, and a small
mess-tin of brandy does for a section. But now there's more brandy
and Cenci divides it up. I draw the rations for my platoon together
with the section commanders. We drink the brandy standing round
the fire. Antonelli swears, Tourn strokes his moustaches, Meschini
grunts. Cenci comes up to us. 'All right, the heavy section?' he says
and gives us something to smoke. God, the army!

Near us I know must be the battalion of Alpini engineers with
men from my home parts, and I go to look for them. I find Vecio
and Renzo. They'd come from the battle where they'd been sig-
nallers for Colonel Signorini. As soon as I saw them walking tired
along the snow I remembered when they'd come to visit me in the
line in September, and my dugout was so well hidden in the wheat
fields that they nearly fell into it together with the motor-cycle they
were riding. It's odd to hear a motor-cycle in a wheat field. There
was no other sound and I, lying in the dugout, was thinking:
'Who can that be?' And it was they, my friends from home, bringing me a sack of flour to make bread with. That day I had some
wine; a month's back rations. Meeting them now makes me feel I'm
in my native village. 'Hallo, Renzo, hallo, Vecio.' 'Mario!' 'Mario!'
They come from the fighting and are tired. 'This time we won't
get home; we'll stay here. The Russians won't let us pass,' says
Vecio. And he's sad. I wonder how many men he's seen die? I
wonder what messages passed over his radio? But Renzo, on the
other hand, is always the same. If he had a flask of wine or heard a
quail singing in the stubble he wouldn't give the bag another
thought. But perhaps he doesn't even think of it now. 'Come along,
cheer up, friends,' I say, 'what a celebration we'll have when we get
back, you'll see, what drunks we'll have! There'll be Scelli too with
his accordion and his girls and his grappa.' But Vecio gives an exhausted smile, though his eyes glitter. I ask them about Rino. They
can't tell me where he is and so I go and look for him. I find the
medical officer of his battalion, who tells me he's seen him a second
before. That cheers me; at least he's alive. I ask his companions
about him. 'He was here just now,' they tell me. I call him and
don't succeed in finding him. Then I meet Adriano and Zanardini:
'Courage,' I say, 'we'll make it.' I return to my platoon, get into an
isba and light a fire. There, I don't know how, I find myself with

Marco of the Nogare, Marco who always put himself out to help anyone and is a friend to all. He too makes me feel better. In my greatcoat pocket I've found a packet of dried vegetables; we melt the snow in our mess-tins and put it on to boil. Then eat together. 'God, the army, Marco!' But we're both of us quite cheerful, and talk about when we emptied a bottle of double Kümmel in Albania. After he's eaten Marco goes back to the runners of Company Headquarters.

How slowly the hours pass; as evening draws near the cold increases. Up there nothing's decided yet and the firing gets sparser and sparser, even the machine-gun bursts seem tired. The sky is all greeny-blue, motionless as the ice, the Alpini talk little to each other and in low voices. Giuanin comes near me, looks at me under the blanket pulled up over his head, says nothing and turns away. I'd like to call him and shout: 'Why don't you ask me if we'll ever get home?' It's cold and night's coming on, the snow and sky look alike. At home at this hour the cows are coming out of their stalls and going to drink in holes broken for them in the iced-up wells. From their stalls comes a steam of manure and the smell of milk; the backs of the cows smoke and the chimneys smoke; the sun reddens everything—the snow, the clouds, the mountains and the faces of the children who are playing with their sledges in the snow; I can see myself among those children; and the houses are warm and the old women sit by the fire mending the children's socks. But even up there in that faraway corner of the steppes there was a warm corner. The snow was pure, the horizon lilac, and the trees rose towards the sky; white and tender birch-trees and under them a group of *isbas*. There couldn't be a war there, they were outside time and the world, everything was as it was a thousand years ago and may be a thousand years hence. I imagined them mending their ploughs and the horses' harness; the old men smoking, the women threading flax. There couldn't be a war under that lilac sky and white birch-trees, among those distant *isbas* in the steppes. I thought: 'I want to go into that warmth too, and then the snow will melt, the birch-trees will become green and I'll watch the earth flower. I'll go out into the steppes with the cows, and in the evening, smoking *macorka*, I'll listen to the quails singing in the wheat fields. In autumn I'll cut the apples and pears to pieces to make syrup and mend the horses' harness and the ploughs and grow old, as if there'd never been a war. I'll forget everything and believe I've always been there.' I looked into the fire, and night fell more and more.

Then I heard an officer calling us on parade, and I smiled: 'On parade the Vestone! On parade the 55th!' The companies, the platoons, the sections lined up. We were to act as rear-guard again. It was night and I didn't understand where we were going. I saw people walking near me and went along with them. Later (how much later?) we stopped near some long low buildings, isolated in the steppes. There we found three or four German tanks and a group of Alpini artillery. The buildings must have been either store-houses or stalls for some Kolkos. Inside it was cold, there was a smell of mules and manure, and tumbled straw on the ground. The stars showed between cracks in the walls. I don't know where the other companies went to; we stopped there. I arranged sentry shifts and put them out for my platoon, lit a fire in a hole with twigs and boiled up a frozen roll of bread. I also found some salt in my pocket.

It was so cold, so cold; the fire made more smoke than flame and my eyes were burning with smoke, cold and lack of sleep. I felt sad, infinitely alone without understanding the cause of my sadness. Perhaps it was the great silence around, the snow, the sky full of stars lost in the snow. But even in such conditions the body did its duty; my legs took me to look for twigs, my hands put them on to the fire and rummaged in my pockets to find the salt to put into the mess-tin. Even the brain did its duty, because afterwards I went and made a round of the sentries ('How are things, Sergeant-major?' 'All right, all right; move about so's not to freeze'), and went to call the new sentries who were to take over. It was as if I were two persons and not one, and one of these was watching what the other did and telling him what to do and what not to do. The strange thing was that both seemed to exist quite physically, as if one could touch the other.

I went to sleep in a big stall. But the best places were taken and so I stretched myself out behind the mules, near their rumps. The place was crammed full of artillery and Alpini and one had to walk over them. I tried to go slowly, to walk lightly, but even so once or twice found myself putting my foot on a frost-bitten limb and then there were shouts and curses. Every now and again I had to go out to see the sentries changed. I'd just come back from one of these inspections, when an artilleryman, walking in the dark, trod with his boots on my face, leaving the marks of nails on my skin. Then I too shouted out at the top of my voice.

We paraded again just before dawn; orders to leave everything except our arms and ammunition. My companions look at me and showing me bundles of letters ask me: 'Can we keep these?' They look gloomy and worried; no one throws any ammunition away. 'Perhaps we're off, finally,' I say to them, 'we'll have to walk a lot and so must be as light as possible.' The officers say: 'Be quick, we're leaving.'

We walk hurriedly along. The stars soon vanish and the sky becomes as it was yesterday. A company of our battalion was missing at the parade and no one knows where it is. Later I heard that the whole of this company was taken prisoner. It was alone in the rearguard and had delayed on its positions that morning. Columns of men in khaki had advanced across the steppes towards them and the officers had said: 'They're the Hungarians coming to take over.' But when they were on top of them they realized they were Russians. So they were caught. The only ones saved were an officer, a soldier or two, and the Captain who caught up with us later. He was drunk with brandy and shouting: 'My company are all prisoners, we're all surrounded, it's useless to fight.' But as he was drunk no one took any notice.

Now it's up to us to go and try and break out of the ring. They say that last night the divisional staff had a conference and decided we're to go on to the very last.

We all became confident, almost gay, we're convinced that we'll make it this time. I sing a song with Antonelli and Tourn. One or two passers-by look at us pityingly; they think we're mad. But we go on singing more gaily than ever. Lieutenant Cenci laughs.

'Forward the Vestone!' we hear a shout. There, now it's up to us. We pass ahead of everyone. The artillerymen open their pouches and give us their cartridges and hand-grenades. They look at us as we looked at those going forward yesterday, trying to encourage us. I laugh with Antonelli and we say: 'Fire accurately now with your 75/13s, right on the target.' 'Don't worry, lads,' they say to us, 'don't worry.'

There, now we should be in it. But why don't the Russians fire? We can see Alpini lying scattered over the snow; they are our comrades of the Verona who'd come to grief yesterday. At the first houses we hear a burst or two of automatic weapons, then nothing more. We turn round to the right and enter an oak-wood. There we sink deep into the snow. In the woods we light a fire with empty ammunition cases. They've told us to wait here. The Russians have an advanced post at another village down below which is a sort of annexe of this one; that's where we have to pass, they keep on saying, because after it there's a good road where the German motorized troops will come and meet us. A Genoese Lieutenant is sent to take over command of my platoon. But he doesn't know how to command anything, at least in this situation, and sows confusion among my men. He keeps one hand always on the butt of his pistol, gesticulates with the other, and shouts: 'You must come with me, I'll lead you back to Italy; I'll shoot anyone who goes off on his own.' And meanwhile he makes no attempt to see that the weapons are working or to check our ammunition. We don't attach much importance either to his gestures or to his words and I go and have a talk to the men. They're cleaning the machine-guns around the fire. I have the two Bredas that are still in working order taken there.

'Forward the Vestone!' we hear again. At the head of the company we see the Captain; I don't know where he's been till now, but there he is ahead of us as always.

Meanwhile a long column is coming from the place we left this morning. Small German Katiuskas are sited at the edge of the wood; I look at those strange weapons with curiosity and think with a slight shudder of the noise they'll make firing. The officers are studying our manœuvre. We of the 55th must make a long detour and take the village almost from the rear. The Valchiese and the battalions of the 5th will go with us; at the last moment the Katiuskas and the German tanks will come into action. We pass drivers making their engines unserviceable and siphoning out the petrol to give it to the tanks. Packets of new mark notes are scattered on the snow, and circulars, lists, registers, etc., drop from broken boxes. I'm pleased to see the end of these things.

I notice Lieutenant Moscioni getting down from a lorry. He

limps over the snow, he's pale, grits his teeth, and comes on looking tall and rigid. I call him and go towards him. He asks at once after his platoon and company; 'There's your platoon, Lieutenant, let's go.' I have so many things to ask him and he me. But we just look at each other, pleased at meeting again.

We walk along in the deep snow, going ahead with difficulty. The weight of our weapons makes us sink in and it's an effort to pull a leg out of the snow and make a step forward. We're all tired and I find it more and more difficult to get other bearers to take over. Lieutenant S—— tries to impose his authority, but I notice that no one listens to him or trusts him; he shouts too much.

I take my turn at carrying the tripod too. There's a lot of sun now, and I sweat. We're out in the open, and in the snow like this must make a fine target. I walk along with my mind suspended, thinking: 'What if they fire mortars at us? We're still too far away for their automatic weapons.' I notice that not all the men of the platoon are following me, my friends notice this too and ask me: 'Why don't they come with us?' 'We're together, cheer up, we'll get through,' I say, 'there are lots of us.' Antonelli swears more and more, as he sinks deeper under the weight of the gun. He's a really fine chap; in spite of his swearing and cursing he always goes on and is nearly always the one who's carrying his section's gun. The Lieutenant, who doesn't like swearing, rebukes Antonelli. Antonelli swears louder than ever and sends him to the devil. How alive the memory is to me!

The other platoons continue to walk along in extended order on our right; we must protect the left of our company, the Russians might come from that side. The Captain is ahead of us all and shouts to us to walk more quickly. I hear Pendoli's voice, Benci's, Moscioni's encouraging their platoons. Suddenly I can feel myself go pale under the crust of earth that covers my face; I've heard mortars being fired. There's the whistle. The bombs pass over our heads and burst fifty yards down below where there's no one. 'Come on, quick, come on,' I say. 'What are we to do?' 'Come on, there's a ditch which we can get along in single file. Come on, quick.' Everyone tries to cluster round me. 'Scatter,' I shout. 'To the left.' There's a long obsessive rumble; I know it well but it doesn't seem as loud as it used to be. I raise my head and then see the trails of the rocket shells going in the direction of the Russians. 'They're ours!' I shout, 'it's the Germans shooting.' We can see *isbas* burning where the shells fall and immediately the Russian mortars stop. Heavy firing can be heard around the first houses in the village; the Valchiese are there, we are ahead of them and must make a wide detour. The Lieutenant, meanwhile, continues to shout, gripping his pistol. He sees Russians everywhere, mistakes even the platoons of our own company for Russians and every hundred yards wants us to set the weapons down and aim them in absurd directions. He's mad, I think, or on the way to becoming so.

Meanwhile, because of the confusion created by the Lieutenant and the time taken in changing the machine-gun bearers, we've got detached from the remaining platoons of our company. The Lieutenant shouts at us from far away: 'Hurry up,' and blames me. He's right about our hurrying, for in case of attack we'd be cut off and unable to give the rifles supporting fire. We put a spurt on. Sweating and cursing we reach a ditch where we can draw breath. On we go again; now we're near the village and about to complete our manœuvre. I see a dark blob on the snow and go up and look; it's an Alpino from the Edolo, he has its green flash. He might be sleeping peacefully; at the last moment he'll have seen the green fields of Val Camonica and heard the cow-bells.

In the village sledges are passing swiftly between the *isbas* and I hear grenades exploding. 'Look,' I shout, 'they're making off.' Another short advance. The detour is over, we've reached the last *isbas* of the village. One must be careful as they are still firing a few yards away. But no; so as not to be surrounded, they've gone off at the last moment after putting up very little resistance. A cloud of stinking black smoke hangs over the village, the *isbas* are burning and corpses are near them; men, women, children. I feel filled with disgust and try to look elsewhere. But my eyes always go back.

We stop to drink by a well and drop our mess-tins in on the long dangling pole. Here we pause.

Colonel Signorini passes near us, there's a smile of satisfaction on his honest face; the manœuvre has come off as if it had been on a parade ground and he says: 'Fine, lads.' We all simultaneously feel a great relief and sense of gaiety. It's over now! A few miles more and we'll be out of the bag. In front of us opens a wide well-used road. The Lieutenant of my platoon says: 'You see what was wanted? We're as good as in Italy, I told you to stick to me.'

We're also joined by the men of my platoon who had left us at the beginning of the action. I reproach them; Antonelli doesn't even look at me. At any rate I can load him up with the gun now. Major Bracchi is jubilant and proud, he's hurrying round reorganizing the Vestone companies. 'Come on, to it! We'll be home eating kid's meat at Easter!'

Meanwhile the head of the column joins us. We learn that Russian tanks have reached where we were this morning. 'They had a real round-up,' they tell us. The Hungarian division had nearly all been taken prisoner, together with those who hadn't the courage or strength to come with us. Now everyone is rushing ahead, creating confusion. But armed men are needed in the vanguard and there are shouts of: 'Forward the Tridentina.' Bracchi cries: 'Vestu! Forward.'

The sun is going down, our shadows lengthen on the snow. Around us is a vast emptiness, without houses, without trees, without any sign of a living being, except for us and the column behind us which merges into the distance where the sky joins the steppe.

We walk on. Looking around I notice that ahead of us, only a little off the track, are some stray horses. I manage to catch them. We try to load the two Bredas on the strongest. But the Captain won't allow us. He says we must always have our weapons ready. And so we lead the horses along behind us and carry the guns. After a bit the Captain takes one of the horses and mounts it. He's very tired and has fever. Cenci takes a horse for his platoon. On the remaining one I load the gun-bearers' packs.

Now the sun has gone down and we're still walking. Mute, with our heads low, we sway as we go, trying to put our feet in the tracks of the man in front. Why are we walking on like this? Just so's to fall in the snow a little farther on and never rise again.

Halt. The man in front stops and we all stop. We fling ourselves down on the snow. Italian and German staff officers on a tracked vehicle near us consult maps and compasses. The hours pass, night comes and we don't move. Perhaps they're waiting for a wireless message. Being motionless we feel the cold worse than ever, and everything round is dark, both steppes and sky. Dry, hard grass sticks out of the snow. The only sound is the strange noise it makes in the wind. None of us speak. We sit on the snow near each other with our blankets on our shoulders. We're ice inside and out, and yet we're still alive. I take my reserve tin of rations out of my pack and open it, but I seem to be chewing ice, it hasn't any taste and won't go down; I manage to eat half and put the rest back in my pack. I get up and bang my feet. Lieutenant Moscioni comes towards me. Cenci is with him and we smoke a cigarette together. We only speak a few words, our vocal chords seem frozen too. But standing like this, smoking, gives a little comfort. We think of nothing, smoke and all is silent. One can't even hear Antonelli swearing.

'Get up! Get up!' comes a shout finally from somewhere. We start off again. It's difficult, very difficult to move the first steps; shoulders ache, legs ache, limbs have gone torpid with the cold and don't seem to obey. But bit by bit, slowly, slowly, the legs begin to carry the body forward.

So once again we walk on; section by section, platoon by platoon. Sleepiness, hunger, cold, exhaustion, the weight of our guns are nothing and everything. The only important thing is to walk. And it's always night, just stars and snow, snow and stars. Looking at the stars I notice that we are changing direction. But where are we going now? I realize we're getting into deep snow again. From the top of a rise we see some lights far away; a village! Antonelli begins to swear again and the Lieutenant to rebuke him and Antonelli to send him to the Verona slums. And Bodei asks me: 'Sergeant-major, will we stop there?' 'Yes, we'll stop,' I reply in a loud voice. But how can I know, I think, if we'll stop or not, or if we'll pass by it or if the Russians are there? 'We'll stop,' I say loudly both for them and myself. Major Bracchi pauses near us: 'Rigoni,' he says, in a voice that everyone can hear. 'We'll find warm *isbas* there, Rigoni.'

But the Russians may be in the village and so we prepare ourselves for an attack. My company is in the vanguard and the Captain gives us our instructions. Platoon by platoon, in extended order, we go slowly down the slope; every now and again I look around to see if the men are following. Three German tanks come with us. Crouching on them are German soldiers dressed in white. Motionless, they grasp their machine-pistols, smoking silently and looking at us. The column has stopped at the top of the slope to see what happens.

Suddenly a black armoured car swerves in at a high speed from our right. It passes in front of us like a ghost and grazes a German tank; then the men on the tank realize that it's Russian. But as it appears, so it vanishes, and in the sky can be seen luminous tracks of tracer bullets following it in vain. It's all happened in such a short time that we're left dazed and incredulous. We start walking towards the village again. At its entrance are two burning haystacks and near them two lorries also burning. These are loaded with ammunition which is exploding and scattering round sparks, flames and shrapnel, like fireworks. As we pass near it we can feel the heat and would like to stop and enjoy this heat from straw, lorries and ammunition burning in the night.

We cross a frozen river deeply set between two steep banks. On the farther bank we stop and wait for the German tanks. There's a hole in the ice, perhaps made by women to get water or by old men to fish in, and we draw up water in our mess-tins. We drink the cold water and wait for the tanks to pass, banging our feet on the ice.

But how can the tanks manage to pass here? We climb up the bank again and some of us enter the first *isba* in the village. But the armoured car of a little while before, the burning lorries and now a strange silence have made us nervous. We talk in low voices thinking the Russians can't be far away. I site our weapons on the edge of the bank. Meanwhile the column has begun moving, coming slowly down towards us like a widening river. We can see the black streaks spreading over the snow. A little higher up there's a little wooden bridge and the tanks try to pass over it one at a time. But they're heavy, the tanks are, and the bridge is small. Will it hold? All our attention is concentrated on the middle of the bridge. The first tank passes slowly. The bridge quivers and creaks all over. Now the others try to pass too. A couple of German soldiers under the bridge on each side watch the tracks and every now and again shout something out. One at a time all the tanks get over.

The head of the column has already reached the *isbas* of the village. The chimneys begin smoking. They'll be boiling their potatoes, some of them will already be sleeping and here we are with our weapons always at the ready. Wouldn't it be better to get into the warmth with them? Who's keeping us here with our arms ready? Why are we doing it? Major Bracchi has gone off with a German officer, and our officers have told us to stay here. Finally someone comes to tell us that we can go into the village too. But then they make us wait again in front of a big red-brick building. Finally we enter it and settle down. Some have found straw, lain down on it and are already asleep. Tardivel and Artico, the corporal of the second rifle platoon, have lit a fire in a corner of a room and are boiling up hard tack with their tinned food. The place is full of smoke, but it's huge and cold; there are two platoons of us inside it. I still have some coffee beans in my greatcoat pocket and grind them up with the handle of my bayonet. I've nothing to eat. In my pack I find a few tablets of solid methylated, light them and try to make myself some coffee with the water I got from the river. But the water refuses to boil, the methylated tablets don't heat enough. I feel sleepy, so sleepy. I can hear my companions already snoring and here I am stubbornly trying to make myself coffee with water that won't boil. The fires have gone out and everyone's sleeping, the icy night enters through the paneless windows, the Alpini lie close to each other for warmth. Rifles and helmets are lined up along the walls. A man complains in his sleep, and another in a corner, alone and sad, is looking at his feet by the light of a piece of candle stuck to the top of his mess-tin; he rubs them slowly then wraps them in pieces of blanket. The water still won't boil and finally I throw it into the coffee-grounds and drink it all. Then I lie down, my feet are like two pieces of marble but I don't want to take my boots off. I twist my legs up to my belly and wrap my arms round my chest. But it's impossible to sleep in this cold.

'Stand to! Stand to!' I hear the Captain calling me. 'Rigoni, get out with the guns at once. Out, all of you!' he shouts and curses. I jump to my feet, I haven't even slept a minute, and yell: 'Wake up! Wake up! Be quick, and keep calm.' There's general confusion. Those who've taken off their boots can't put them on again because their feet have swollen and the boots are hard as wood. Some are looking for their rifles and others for their helmets, one is still in a heavy sleep and I shake him hard.

The confusion's worse on the stairs and in the passages. They're crowded with artillerymen of the Valcamonica; it's difficult to pass without treading on someone who won't get up, and lies there complaining. We parade outside in front of the building. Many men are missing and it's impossible to tell where they are; one of our guns is also missing but it's the one that doesn't work. The Captain goes into the building and finds the missing gun in the big room. When he comes down he blames me. 'Captain,' I say, 'I'd left it there because it doesn't work. It's all broken and is a useless weight to carry. Look at the state we're in. We've got very little ammunition too.' But the Captain won't accept these arguments and I go up myself to fetch it.

Moscioni's, Cenci's, Pendoli's platoons have already vanished, swallowed up in the dark, in different directions. With the Lieutenant, who's full of bravado, we move with the three heavy machineguns towards the last houses on the left of the village. I keep the men of the platoon close together and go up and down like a sheepdog. 'Come on, Bodei, on with you, Tourn, walk, Bosio; bring the ammunition cases ahead,' and so we reach the place the Captain's assigned to us. Who knows what's happened, perhaps the Russians are attacking. I can't get any idea of the situation. Every now and again we hear firing on our right. We site our guns; one at the corner of an *isba* and one in front of a little mound. I aim them in two different directions, instinctively, towards the steppes. It's still night, perhaps two in the morning, the sky is slowly covering over and the moon which is going down behind us lights up the steppes ahead of us between a rent in the clouds. When it comes out I tell the men to get into the shadows.

The Lieutenant goes into the nearest *isba*. They are poor *isbas*, poorer than usual, small and cold even to look at. But the Lieutenant comes quickly out with his pistol in his hand. He shouts for me to run to him. I enter the *isba* with a grenade in my hand. Inside are two women and two children, and he orders me to tie them up. I think the Lieutenant must really be losing his reason. The women and children have understood and look at me with terrified eyes. They turn to me weeping and talking Russian. What voices those women and children had! Like the sorrow and hope of all humanity, and the revolt against all evil. I take the Lieutenant by an arm and we go out. Still grasping his pistol he enters another *isba*. I follow him.

Here I find some disbanded soldiers of the Vicenza Division. They are crouching under the table, unarmed, numb and terrified. An old man is lying on an iron bedstead. The Lieutenant shouts to me: 'He's a partisan, kill him!' The poor old man looks at me, sighing and trembling so much that the whole bed shakes. 'Tie him up, if you don't want to kill him,' the Lieutenant shouts at me again. Antonelli has come into the *isba* and seen everything. The Lieutenant points to a piece of rope in a corner. He really is mad. I lean slowly down to get the rope; Antonelli takes the covers off the old man and I go up to him. The old man! The old man is a poor paralytic, and I throw away the rope and say to the Lieutenant: 'He's not a partisan! He's a paralytic.' The Lieutenant leaves the *isba*, he still seems to have a gleam of reason left. Those poor devils from the Vicenza are still lying under the table, terrified, and I ask them if they'd like to come with me. 'I don't trust you; I don't trust you,' they repeat. And there they stay. I go out with Antonelli and leave all those wretches in peace.

Under the place where the machine-gun is set, right under the earth, I hear whispering. There's a trap-door. It's one of those holes where the Russians put their provisions for the winter, a kind of cellar near their *isbas*. I pull up the trap-door. Down below we see a light and women and children huddled close together. They climb up the ladder and come out one at a time with their arms raised. I feel like smiling, but the children are crying. How many of them are there? They keep on coming out. Antonelli laughs and says: 'There's an ants' nest down there.' I send all these people into the *isbas*, where they hurry off happily. Luckily for them the Lieutenant hasn't noticed anything. Some time later a little boy brings us some hot boiled potatoes.

A couple of shells pass whistling over our heads and explode at the other end of the village. I notice two columns of men coming out of the steppe towards us. Russians or our own stragglers? They're still a long way off and it's dark. Every now and again the moon comes out and lights up the steppe but now it's completely black. The Lieutenant has returned. He too has noticed the groups coming towards us. Perhaps he's come back for that. 'Fire!' he says. 'Fire!

Go on, fire.' 'No,' I say, 'don't fire; be calm, don't make any noise.'

The weapons are sighted, the Lieutenant keeps on saying: 'Fire, fire I tell you.' And I, 'No. We must wait for them to get nearer, we've very little ammunition and anyway they may be Italians or Germans.' The few men remaining from the fifty of the platoon still trust me and don't fire. 'The Lieutenant's mad,' says Antonelli. 'He's mad,' says someone else. 'Why fire? There's no need to.'

There's firing in the village. What's happening now? Stray bullets pass wailing between the gardens and the *isbas*; but our corner is calm.

Ramazzini, an intelligent runner from Collio V. T., comes hurrying up and gasps out: 'Quick, Rigoni, be quick, you must join the rest of the company.'

Like shadows we dismount the guns, hoist them up with the ammunition on our shoulders and, in single file, without saying a word, return towards the brick building. Not one of our men's there. The company has left without waiting for us.

The village is all in confusion; sledges colliding, officers shouting, people coming and going in every direction. We walk quickly along the sides of the track to get ahead and join our company. But it's hard work because we have to cleave our way over fresh snow. Shells explode in front and behind us, sometimes hitting the middle of the column. But we feel as cold and apathetic about the shells as about the lice.

A grey and livid dawn comes, it begins to snow. I look back, there are very few of us left, ten perhaps; but we still have our weapons with us, and only a case or two of ammunition is missing. The Lieutenant isn't there either—who knows where he's been left? We're still walking along the flank of the column, by the edge of a fir-wood; we're all white with snow like the firs. A German, an airman by his uniform, is walking slowly ahead of us, his feet wrapped in rags; we pass him, and also some sledges with Germans and Hungarians in them.

Now everyone has stopped because there's firing at the head of the column. We go on. Farther on we find the Alpini artillerymen; so we're among our own people; forward again then. Finally we reach our company. The Captain sees us arrive and doesn't say anything. We all stop; the Valchiese is in the vanguard. Our heavies can be heard firing and the Bergamo group get their guns ready. To pass we have to take another village. But there's not much firing. We start walking slowly on, it's almost restful now. One or two more of our platoon join us. Here and there on the snow are empty cartridge cases, black marks of explosions, tank tracks.

The village faces east, behind a rise. It slopes down towards a ditch and is surrounded by fruit-trees. Dogs can be heard barking in the thick snowy air. The Major passes among us and says: 'We'll rest here; go into the *isbas*, eat and sleep; perhaps we'll leave to-morrow morning.' To be able to rest for a whole night seems un-believable. In the warmth all night!

I choose a fine looking *isba* towards the middle of the village. We enter and stack our weapons, which are encrusted with snow and ice, by the fire. We go into another *isba* and take three chickens from it (it's not right, I think, for us to take them from the *isba* we're staying in, others can come along later and take the ones there). As the village is on a slope and we're on a dominating point from above we see those arriving. Alpini from my company are chasing a pig which is zigzagging over the snow like a bat. They fire at it with their rifles, and finally catch and kill it. They're running about, shouting and laughing, as if it were a fiesta day.

We come back into the *isba* to pluck the chickens among calls of delight from the woman there. Water is put on to boil; one man fetches straw to lie on, another wood.

Finally we sit down on benches round the fire. It's lovely to see the fire; we feel good, content and think of nothing. But even here we can't be left in peace. The Captain comes in. 'Rigoni, what are you doing here?' he says to me, and the spell breaks. He looks at the chickens, the fire, the straw, the wood. 'What are you doing here?' he repeats. Then batmen, quartermasters and runners come in. 'Rigoni, go with your men and weapons to that *isba*.' And through the open door and the falling snow the Captain points one out to me at the bottom of the slope. 'Go down there and site the weapons in that direction,' and he points. He says: 'There may be an attack at any moment; by partisans or troops. Site your weapons and take it in turn to rest and warm up.' He keeps the warm *isba* and the fire and the straw for himself and doesn't even let us take the chickens. Antonelli swears and the others curse too as they follow me. This is worse than going into an attack. We reach the bottom of the village. The *isba* is cold and empty. We site the guns and try to arrange ourselves as best we can. But it's snowing and the weapons get encrusted with ice at once. If we go on like this, we won't be able to fire them at all in the end, and so someone brings them inside and we put them between the outer and inner doors of the *isba*, with the barrel pointing towards the steppes.

Then the Captain sends us down two chickens and we cook them in our mess-tins. They'll leave us in peace now. I stop at the door and watch it snowing and hear the sound of engines in the air. Aeroplanes. They're flying low but in the snow one can't make out if they're ours or Russian. The noise gets louder. I clearly see dark objects detaching from the planes and then parachutes opening. I run to warn the Captain, thinking they may be Russian parachutists. There are lots of them and they are coming slowly down on the rise in front of us, beyond the fruit-trees. The Captain looks and doesn't know what to say. Immediately, however, we hear that they aren't Russian parachutists, but ammunition, medicine, and petrol containers dropped by the Germans.

I return to my platoon, the two chickens are cooked and we divide them into fifteen parts. But even now we can't be in peace; a sledge has stopped in front of us loaded with wounded from the Bergamo Division. A Captain asks me for hospitality. 'The other *isbas* are all occupied,' he says, 'let us in. We're wounded.' Meanwhile another sledge full of wounded has arrived, so we leave them our places and the soup from the chickens.

We try to settle down in a small stall nearby, but it's open to the four winds. The Captain sends to tell us that another platoon from another company is now in position not far away to protect the village, and that we can withdraw. But where can we go at this hour of the night? It's all dark. We knock at a number of *isbas*. They're all occupied. Finally we manage to find our own riflemen. They give us hospitality. But we can't all fit in; on the table, under the table, on the benches, under the benches, above the stove, on the ground. I have to content myself with remaining on foot near the stove. But it's torture outside now, and here it's warm. The *isba* is soaked with steam, smoke and smells. Tardivel asks me if I've eaten. They've killed a pig, and he gives me some liver cooked with onions in the pig's own fat. It's incredible how good the liver is and what a good companion Tardivel seems; he's done three years in Africa out of eight with the Alpini.

Cenci, who's in an *isba* opposite this one with his platoon, sends to tell me that if we're too many of us in here some of us can go to his. Four of us do so.

I lie down under the table, stretch my legs and feel that I could never be so comfortable anywhere in the world as here. The oil-lamp dims; Cenci talks in a low voice to some soldier; I can hear the straw rustling, the fire in the stove crackling and the calm snoring of those who had gone to sleep before. And I think of a big moon lighting a lake, a road all lined by sweet-scented gardens, a warm voice, a tinkling laugh and the sound of waves on a shore. It's even better here, outside it's hell and so I fall asleep.

There's a knocking; knocking at the door. Not in a rough way, but gently, as if we were in a town; though insistently. Someone wakes up and curses. Lieutenant Cenci says: 'Who can it be?' The knocking goes on and one can hear the wind through it. I get up in the dark and go to open the door. An Italian soldier, with bare head and without a greatcoat, is looking calmly at me. He says quietly: 'Good evening, sir. Is your father at home?' I look at him fixedly. 'Good evening,' I say. 'D'you want to come in?' And he: 'Is your father in?' 'Yes,' I say: 'but he's asleep. What d'you want?' 'I've come about the articles,' he replies, 'will you please see about publishing them? I'll return when your father's up. Good-bye. I'll be back later.' And he goes quietly off, his head bent and his hands behind his back, and vanishes into the wind and the night. When I re-enter the *isba* Cenci says to me: 'Who was it?' 'Someone looking for my father, he had some articles to publish, he'll come back later, sir, good evening.' Cenci looks at me in silence and watches me until I've stretched out again under the table.

We wake up with a jump; a bullet has shattered the glass and buried itself in the wall above my hand. 'Stand to! Stand to!' we hear shouts. 'The partisans!' We creep out. Shadows are running about here and there; bullets are buzzing about like wasps. I get under a hedge near the *isba* and wait to see what happens. Nearby there's a flash in my direction. I hear the bullet pass over me, then jump to one side, fire in the direction of the flash and jump again.

Silence. Then I hear talking. They're Italians. Luckily I haven't hit anyone. I call out, they reply and go away. God knows what's happening; I wait there alone and motionless; men are coming from the other side of the ditch shouting: 'Italians, don't fire. *Deutsche Soldaten!* Don't fire. *Kamarad.*' They are Germans who'd been mistaken for partisans. But there may also have been some partisans too. We re-enter the *isbas*, sleep for another hour, and then dawn comes.

I can't remember the order in which things happened since that dawn. I only remember the single episodes, the faces of my companions, the cold. Certain things are clear and limpid. Others like nightmares. The cadences of Bracchi's voice rallying us: 'Come on!' or giving orders: 'Forward, Vestone! Forward the Bergamo group! Forward the Morbegno!'

It's morning, and the column divides in two. The Vestone is advance-guard for the left-hand column. Our company is at the head. There's a fine sun and it's not cold. We see some vehicles coming off the road towards us and then stop a certain distance away. The officers look at them through their binoculars; they're Russian. At once some German anti-tank guns are brought up, hurriedly aimed and fired. The vehicles vanish into the steppes as they came. A short time afterwards, perhaps half an hour, as we go over the top of a rise, we are greeted by the heavy fire of automatic weapons. From down in the village the Russians can only see our heads showing and fire at them. The bullets pass high. We turn back ten yards or so and wait. The other companies of the Valchiese arrive and a German half-track with senior officers on it. Now we'll have to capture this village in order to pass.

We go back up the rise and down the other side towards the village. The Valchiese on our right. The other companies of the Vestone on our left.

The Russians begin firing again. Tourn, who's walking a pace or two behind me, is wounded in the hand. He shouts to me: 'I'm wounded!' and turns back dangling his hand, which is dripping blood on the snow. I shout to disperse. The Russian fire is heavy. We lie down on the snow in the open, and then go on down the slope. A little to our right, behind a haystack, is the Captain with a recce section. I join them with those who are following me. There is very heavy firing in the direction of the haystack and when we manage to join them we heave a sigh of relief. Sheltered behind it, we test the heavy machine-gun, take it to pieces, clean it, work the cocking-handle energetically and test the recoil. The bullets continue to pass at the sides of the haystack and a runner, Ramazzini, sent by Moscioni with a note to the Captain, falls groaning as soon as he gets into the open. Two men from his section go out to fetch him. They carry him to safety among bullets which are still whistling. He's been hit in the stomach and now lies groaning on the snow near us.

We hear some shells go off and then watch them explode among the *isbas* in the village; they're our 75/13s and we don't seem alone any more. Now the heavy machine-gun is in working order and I go out in front of the haystack with Antonelli. We set it up in a kind of low trench of snow there and return behind the haystack to get the ammunition. The whole village lies before us now. Antonelli and I are at the gun. The others are behind the haystack or lying motionless on the snow farther back. We fire at some sledges which are passing swiftly between one hedge and another and at a group of Russian soldiers entering an *isba*. Their surprise is obvious. But now they've seen us and started firing themselves. Our comrades begin to advance again. Level with us on the right, the Valchiese are struggling slowly over the snow and the Russians are firing at them. We can hear the bursts. Alpini drag themselves slowly back, helping each other along. I put in a cartridge-belt and take aim. Antonelli fires. From behind the haystack the Captain shouts: 'Fire! Fire! Fire!' But we've finished our ammunition and shout for more. Bodei, Giuanin and Menegolo run crouching towards us with three cases of three hundred rounds. A big case of ammunition, which the drivers of the 54th had, has arrived behind the haystack. They run crouching because the Russians are firing really heavily; I go towards them to help.

Lieutenant Cenci is watching the village through his binoculars and shouts from thirty yards away: 'Rigoni, quick! There are Russians passing in groups under that bridge at the beginning of the village. They're leaving. You can see them as soon as they come out the other side of the bridge. I'll tell you when they go in and then be ready to fire. There they are.' I can see the Russians come running out from under the bridge, and still see them for a few yards before they jump into a ditch. We aim the gun at the space they have to pass, which is about three hundred yards from us. Cenci shouts: 'Now, Rigoni!' And Antonelli whose eyes are fixed on the spot, fires. Cenci shouts: 'Now!' Antonelli fires and I feed another belt in. The Russians are running. But they're firing at us too. And the bullets pass very close to us. Two hit the gun; on the legs of the tripod and under the sights; and bullets plunge into the snow in front, beside and behind us, raising little clouds of spray. Antonelli curses; the heavy's stuck. I get up to my feet and open the cover of the gun. Nothing much. Antonelli swears and says to me: 'Get down or they'll kill you.' We begin firing again and I pile the ammunition cases on top of each other in front of me. 'They're some sort of cover,' I think.

Twenty yards or so behind us is the vanished Lieutenant; the one who was supposed to be commanding our platoon. I hear him calling out and groaning. He's wounded in a leg. I shout to him to get back. But he doesn't move. Then two soldiers from our company go and fetch him, and I never saw him again. I know his wounded leg got gangrene and he died on a sledge, and now I think that perhaps he was not such a bad fellow after all.

The rifle platoons lying on the snow a little behind us get up and fix their bayonets. The ones from the Valchiese go down the hill and so do the others farther along. Our Captain is among the leaders and shouts orders as he clutches a Russian parabellum. We start moving ourselves but the gun is red hot and Antonelli burns his hands trying to take it by the barrel. Now the other men from our platoon join us. The Russians are not expecting a hand-to-hand and make off. We set the heavy machine-gun down again and fire at them as they retreat. We're at the first *isbas* and throw some hand-grenades. Meanwhile the German tanks come grinding down the hill. On the ground I find a red disk, one of those used for traffic, and begin waving this towards the tanks to show they can go ahead. The Germans pass laughing. As soon as they enter the village the troops on the tanks jump nimbly to the ground and I watch their method of occupying the *isbas*. They give the door a kick, jump to one side, aim their machine-pistols and then very slowly look inside.

When they see any heaps of straw they fire a shot or two into them; and scrutinize dark corners and cellars with torches.

I begin going round the village alone. The civilians have nearly all vanished. Our soldiers don't enter the *isbas* as the Germans do. They open doors and cross thresholds unsuspectingly. I fall in with a platoon of Alpini engineers. It's a surprise to see them there and I ask them about Rino. 'He's here with us,' they tell me, 'or at least was until a moment ago.' And as I talk to them I see Rino running across the road. He sees me too; we call and fall into each other's arms. His helmet is clamped down on his head, and his rifle clutched in one hand as he grasps me round the neck with the other. Rino! He makes me see all my youth in front of me, my home, my dear ones. We were at school together. I remember what he was like as a boy and feel like asking him why he's grown. But I can't get a word out. I feel his keenness, his anxiety to make himself useful, to help those who can't and even those who won't do things, and then I find myself alone again. I don't know how it's happened, and go into an *isba* and come out again.

A German on horseback gallops through the village shouting: '*Ruski Panzer! Ruski Panzer!*' Behind him comes the sound of engines. I can even hear the clanging of the tracks. I go pale and long to make myself small enough to jump into a mouse-hole. I get behind a fence and through the cracks see the tanks passing less than a yard's distance away. I hold my breath. On every tank are Russian soldiers clutching automatic weapons. It's the first time I've seen them in battle so close. They're young and haven't got evil faces, only serious and pale ones, set and wary. They've got padded trousers and jackets. On their heads are the usual big caps with the red star on them. Should I have fired? There were three tanks, they passed one after the other grazing the fence, fired a burst or two at random and then disappeared. I rushed towards an *isba*. Inside were three girls. They were young, and smiled, hoping by this to induce me not to take anything. I found some milk and drank a little of it; and in a chest, three tins of jam, some biscuits and butter. All Italian stuff taken, perhaps, from some abandoned dump. The three girls were now almost crying, and standing round imploringly. I tried to explain to them that this was Italian and not Russian stuff, and so I could take it, and that I was hungry and my comrades were hungry too. But the girls were so tearful, and looked so sad, that I left them a tin of jam and a small packet of butter. Then I went out with the rest, munching a biscuit. The three girls looked at the ground and said: '*Spaziba*.'

Outside I was just in time to see the last shells being exchanged between the Russian and German tanks. While I was in the *isba* I'd heard nothing. The girls had made me forget the war for an instant. Later I learnt that the horseman who'd passed shouting just before had warned the German tanks, which were in position just outside the village. And the Russian tanks were now all burning; the signs of the short battle showed on the snow; marks of wild turns, vicious twists and sudden stops, and black splodges of oil and other things. A tank had been hit in the tracks, and they lay on the snow like two black stripes on white paper; sad, like stumps of a living thing. Corpses were burning near the tanks. Some Russian soldiers had fallen into the snow from a tank. A German crawled cautiously up to them and fired at their backs from a few inches away. The other Germans, a short way off, were taking photographs and laughing, waving their arms and talking, pointing to the marks of battle on the snow. But suddenly from one of the burning Russian tanks a burst of automatic fire went off in the direction of the Germans, who quickly scattered like a flock of birds. Two of them jumped on their tank and fired a shot at the Russian tank, which, hit in the ammunition reserve, blew up as one sees sometimes on the cinema. I was watching this incident from a short way off; all the Russians whom I'd seen passing from behind the fence were now dead there, in the snow.

The Alpini from my platoon and others had all collected nearby and I joined them. I distribute the bits of food I'd found in the *isba* and spread some butter and jam for myself on a biscuit. The Captain sees this, calls me and rebukes me in front of everyone, because, he says, this isn't the moment for eating or thinking of eating; and he makes me put everything away. Perhaps the Captain's got fever; I don't reply, and draw to one side. Then the Captain calls me and says: 'Give me something to eat too.'

We leave the village. I meet Rino again. 'I've drunk a pailful of milk,' he says, and smiles.

We cross a frozen marsh. There are clumps of high stiff grass that could hide an ambush, and we proceed cautiously. My company is leading; Cenci's and Pendoli's sections go first, and we come immediately after; behind are the other companies of the Vestone, the other two battalions of the 6th, the mountain batteries of the 2nd, and then the interminable lines of disbanded Italians, Hungarians, Germans; wounded, frozen, starving, unarmed.

A Russian tank appears on top of a rise and fires a shot or two at the column, but a 75/13 of the 19th replies quickly and the tank disappears. Major Bracchi, our Captain, a German officer, and an artillery Major are just behind me and shout out orders from time to time. We near a group of buildings, storehouses for grain perhaps. From one of these we see people coming out waving their arms, shouting at us and running towards us. 'They're ours, they're ours,' we shout. We think of many things but the strongest is; they're Italians, Italian soldiers coming to meet us from the other side. 'We're out of the bag,' we think. We all become gay. I feel like turning somersaults in the snow. Antonelli shouts and sings. We walk light-heartedly towards them, feeling as if we're on air. But the illusion only lasts a few minutes. When we're near them we realize they're unarmed. They want to embrace us. There are about a hundred of them. In the confusion we learn, in a few words, that they'd been prisoners of the Russians, that they'd seen the battle going in our favour through the cracks of the stockade where they were confined, and that the Russian sentries had made off at our approach. We want to know more, but Bracchi cuts them short and sends them to the back of the column.

Evening falls and we're still walking over the snow. We see some Italian soldiers lying rigid close beside each other. From the colour of their flashes I note that they belong to the Alpini engineers of the Cuneo Division. The track is now hard and shiny with ice polished by the wind. I'm carrying the 37 mm. Breda on my shoulders and keep slipping and falling. I get up, then fall again. How often did this happen? The company has closed up its ranks and we're walking quickly. Major Bracchi comes beside me, and looks at me in silence. It's night; we're still walking and I'm still falling. Then I drop behind and Bracchi says to me: 'Come on, we'll make it.' But how far is it still? Now our General's here too. He passes us on a German vehicle, stops and looks at us: 'Good lads, good lads,' he says. From the vehicle he watches us pass one by one. Afterwards he comes up again, walks a bit with us and shouts: 'A few more hours and then we'll be out, a few miles away there's a German strongpoint.'

One of my comrades finally takes over the gun from me. We change direction. The officers have become serious; they're saying among themselves that a Russian column has infiltrated between us and the German strongpoint. It's dark when we stop for the night in a village. We can't manage any more, are desperate with exhaustion, cold, hunger, lack of sleep. Our boots are like glass on the snow. We feel in our pockets the letters we can't send off. 'Come on, to it.' Milk and polenta in a warm kitchen. 'Shall we ever get home?' Go on, courage. And I fall down. But now we've reached a village.

The German tanks stop at the first *isbas*, we go to the last. The *isbas* are empty and the village deserted. The doors are locked. We have to break in. In the *isba* we enter the stove is still tepid, but there's no one there. It's warm and clean; the wick is still burning in front of the ikon and there are curtains in the windows and hangings and photographs on the walls.

Some of us bring in some wood and straw. In the stall nearby are two piglets and a big one. The piglets we give to the other platoons and kill the big pig for ourselves.

An officer is sent to command our platoon who has the reputation of having the evil eye. He comes into the *isba*, stands up in the middle with both hands in his pockets, and begins to give orders. He wants the straw to be evenly scattered, the blankets smooth and in line, the floor clean, and the pig cooked in such and such a way. He's tall and stiff with hard eyes. He continues to give orders. But my comrades are more sensible than he is, they don't reply, say nothing and continue to go on as they always have ever since I've been with them. 'Tomorrow morning,' I think, 'I'll go to the Captain, or if that's not enough, to the Major, or the Colonel. I don't want this officer in my platoon. I can deal with it myself. Unless they send me someone like Moscioni or Cenci.'

I hear that Rino is in an *isba* nearby and go and call him. I'd like him with me, tonight. Then I roast a piece of pork on the embers and we eat it together, sitting on the straw. Finally we lie down covered with our blankets and greatcoats. The warmth passes from one body to the other, the breath of one warms the other's face, every now and again we half open our eyes and look at each other. Memories bring a lump to my throat. I'd like to talk about our homes, our dear ones, our girls, our mountains, and our friends. D'you remember, Rino, the time the French teacher said to us; a rotten pear can make a healthy pear go bad, but a healthy pear can't make a rotten pear healthy? And I was the rotten pear and you the healthy one. D'you remember, Rino? And how I always got bad marks. There are so many things I'd like to say to you and I can't even wish you good night. Our companions are all asleep already and we aren't. Outside are the desolate steppes and the stars shining above this *isba* are the same which shine above our homes. We fall asleep.

In the morning I go to the Captain and explain about my platoon. He talks to the Major about it. The new officer is sent away and I shan't see him any more. He'll have gone to act the hero amongst the stragglers. So from now on I'll be left alone in command of the platoon. The twenty remaining men are pleased and so am I; Antonelli most of all.

The sun warms our aching limbs from a clear sky and we're still walking. What day is it today? And where are we? There aren't any dates or days of the week any more. Just us walking.

Passing through a village we see some corpses in front of the door of an *isba*. They're women and children. Perhaps they were caught in their sleep, for they're in their chemises. Their bare legs and arms are like lilies on an altar. One woman is lying naked on the snow, whiter than the snow, which is red near her. I don't want to look, but they're there even if I don't. A young woman is lying with her arms open; she has a white line on her face. Why that? Who did it? And we go on walking.

We pass another narrow deserted valley. We walk along it, anxiously; I feel as if I'm suffocating and wish we were out of it. I look everywhere apprehensively, listen and hold my breath. I'd like to run. At any moment I expect to see the turrets of tanks appear and hear bursts of machine-gun fire. But we pass through.

I'm hungry. When did I eat last? I don't remember. The column passes between two villages a mile or so apart. There's sure to be something to eat there. Little groups detach themselves from the column and set off towards the villages in search of food. The officers shout at them, tell them there might be partisans or red patrols there. Some soldiers from my platoon also go off in search of food. During a short halt we stop for a drink at a well and then I go off to what seems the nearest *isba*. But it's one of the biggest and has already been visited by many others. All I find is a handful of dried apples which the Russians use to make syrup.

We are still walking and night's coming on. It's cold; colder than ever, perhaps forty degrees. The breath freezes on our beards and moustaches; we walk on in silence with our blankets pulled up over our heads. We stop. There's nothing. No trees, no houses, just the snow and the stars and us. I fling myself down on the snow; and even the snow doesn't seem to be there; I close my eyes on nothingness. Perhaps death will be like this, or perhaps I'm sleeping. I'm in a white cloud. But who's calling me? Who's shaking me so violently? Let me be. 'Rigoni! Rigoni! Rigoni! Get up. The column's left. Wake up. Rigoni.' It's Lieutenant Moscioni calling me anxiously, and I see him bending over me as I open my eyes. He gives me another couple of shakes and now I can see his face clearly, and his two dark eyes fixed on me, his beard hard and shiny with white frost, a blanket over his head. 'Rigoni, take these,' he says. And he gives me two little pills. 'Swallow them, come along, make an effort.' I get up, walk along with him and gradually we catch up with the company and I understand what's happened . . . How many have thrown themselves down on the snow and never got up again? Cenci and Moscioni make me mount a horse. But it's worse than waking up; I'm frightened of getting frost-bite, dismount and walk on. Cenci gives me a cigarette and we smoke. 'Say, Rigoni, what would you like most now?' I smile, and they do too. They know the reply because I've said it at other times, walking along at night. 'To get into a house, into a house like ours at home, take off all my clothes, be without boots, or pouches, without a blanket on my head; have a bath and put on a linen shirt, drink a cup of coffee, and then throw myself on to a bed, but a real bed with mattress and

sheets, a big bed in a warm room with an open fire; and then sleep
and sleep and sleep; wake up, then, and hear the sound of bells and
find a table laid; wine, spaghetti, fruit, grapes, cherries, figs; then
go back to sleep and hear music.' Cenci laughs, Antonelli laughs,
and my companions also laugh. 'I'll do that too, if I return,' says
Cenci, 'and then a month by the sea, on the sand, all naked on the
sand, alone with the sun burning into me.' Meanwhile we walk on
and Cenci sees the green sea and I a real bed. But Moscioni looks
serious, he's more conscious of things than us, he has his feet on the
ground and sees steppes, Alpini, mules, snow. Down there is a light.
It's not a green sea, it's not a real bed, it's only a village.

But that light is like the one in the fairy tale. It gets farther away.
We never reach it. The village is small and there's no room for all of
us; we're among the first, but the *isbas* are already full. Perhaps
we'll have to spend the rest of the night in the open. The Captain,
Cenci, Moscioni and half the already reduced company go in search
of billets. I remain with the rest of the men and my platoon.

The morning after the Captain told me that he'd sent a runner to
say there was room for all of us with them. But I never saw any
runner arrive that night. Some of my companions settled down
round a haystack, covering themselves with hay. Others went off
somewhere or other, and I remained with Bodei by a fire. Suddenly
we heard bleating and Bodei got up, went to get the sheep which
had bleated and killed it in front of the fire. I helped him skin it
and we began roasting a leg each over the open fire. The hot juicy
flesh was incredibly good. And after the legs we roasted the heart,
the liver, the kidneys, all on our bayonets. The flesh roasting on the
fire made the air thick and good. We ate the legs, and the hours
passed, then we ate the shoulders and the back legs. A couple of
Italian infantrymen and a German joined us, perhaps attracted by
the smell; they finished up the sheep, and even gnawed over the
bones which Bodei and I had left. They had no weapons and wore
rags and straw tied round their feet with wire instead of boots. We
made a bit of room for them round the fire, and they sat there
silently. Bodei grumbled for they didn't even get up to go and look
for wood; they didn't even bother to move their heads out of the
smoke.

I felt so sleepy. I slept but the dawn soon came, and a short time after it the sounds which always preceded the column's departure. I collect my platoon together. We set off, but the column, instead of moving forward, goes back on yesterday's tracks. What's happening? Down on the right we see quite a big village. They say the Russians are there and that we'll have to capture it so as to leave the way open for the others following behind. 'Forward the Vestone!' they shout ahead, and let us pass; yes, now they're ready to let us pass. We're told where to attack and go at it once again. Cenci's and Moscioni's platoons are on the right, mine in the centre and a bit to the rear with the heavy machine-gun, then the other companies of the battalion, and finally the Germans. Some Russian soldiers come out of a ditch with their hands up and our men disarm them. A shot or two can be heard, but faintly. Major Bracchi follows us and every now and again shouts orders. We see other Russian soldiers going off. It doesn't seem a real battle. The heavy machine-gun hasn't fired a single shot. Being higher up we can see everything. We reach the first *isbas* and go round the village, find a flock of geese squawking, grab some, twist their necks and throw them over our shoulders, carrying them by the heads. So the battle was for the geese. They're shouting for us to collect in the middle of the village, where the church is. It's already over.

Going in the direction of the church we see some abandoned lorries of American make; there are also guns sited with ammunition beside them. Odd that the Russians should have so much artillery in a little village. But why haven't they fired? It was a well-armed strongpoint. Last night the column passed along the verge of the rise which runs above the village. It was there I fell asleep in the snow. They hadn't heard us. We'd been like shadows. And I remembered having seen a light or two nearby; and someone saying: 'Why don't we go there?' As I think of these things I see an *isba* with the door open and go inside. I don't notice that on my way in I've kicked a corpse, a Russian, lying across the threshold. In the *isba* I look around for something to eat. Someone has been here before me; I see drawers pulled out, sheets and lace spread over the floor, and chests open. I search about in a drawer, but then see some women and children crying in a corner. They are sobbing loudly with their heads in their hands and their shoulders shaking. Then I notice the dead man across the door and see that near him the floor is all red with blood. I can't describe what I felt; shame or self-contempt, sorrow for them or for myself. I rushed outside as if I were guilty.

Our men are collecting again. This time in front of the church. Abandoned Italian lorries can be seen loaded with dried potatoes cut in slices, and I fill my pockets with these. On the snow there are also two barrels of wine. One is broached with the wine all frozen inside in red scales. I fill my mess-tin with the scales and then put some in my mouth. An officer says: 'Be careful, it might be poisoned.' But it's not poisoned at all.

The Germans are taking all the Russian prisoners we've made; they go off with them, then we hear a number of bursts of fire and a single shot or two. It's snowing.

We begin walking again. The units are getting mixed up with each other. A strong cold wind blows up. We're all white. The wind whistles among the dry grass, the snow makes our faces smart. We hang on to each other. The artillery mules sink in to their bellies, jib and refuse to go on. Curses, shouts, screams in the torturing wind.

Another night in another village. Aren't they *isbas* down there near those trees? I walk off alone in their direction, sink deep into the snow up to my chest and go on as if I were swimming, dreaming of an *isba*. I reach the point where I thought the *isbas* were and find only shadows. Shadows of what? I go back. But again I have the impression of seeing *isbas*; and go off in their direction until I reach a river-bank. But there's nothing there either, only three birch-trees loaded with icicles raising their branches furry with icicles to the starry sky. And I sob on the river-bank. Where are my comrades? Will I have the strength to return to them? I find them again in a brick building. The village was only a few hundred yards away and I'd been walking in the opposite direction. It's cold and the bit of fire we've lit gives out more smoke than anything else. Most of the room is filled with great heaps of grain. We lie down on the grain, still covered with snow and with our blankets frozen stiff. It's days and days since I've taken my boots off and now I do so to melt the ice on them and dry them. My feet swell up at once. I don't take the socks off for fear of seeing my feet blue and the skin flaking away. I go to sleep. A sudden flash and exploding grenades wake us up with a start. 'Now we're for it,' I think. I can't get my boots on, which are hard as wood. I grasp my rifle and snatch my grenades. Some men are shouting, others crying, one breaks a window-pane and jumps down barefoot on to the snow in the road. I slide along the heap of grain and get behind a window. There's a great fire, the village is all lit up. I see people running between the flames, others flinging themselves in the snow. Lieutenant Pendoli comes in to us: 'It's not an attack,' he shouts, 'it's not partisans. The fires lit by our men to warm themselves have set fire to the church, and the ammunition in there's gone off.' The explanation produces calm again and we settle down on the grain once more. A terrible cold is coming in through the broken window and the snow looks all red as if it were soaked with blood.

What day is it today? I see a fine sun and a pink sky. It's like one of those March days which herald spring. Days full of hope. We stop, there's a short halt. With Tourn, Antonelli and Chizzarri I sing in Piedmontese: 'In the shadow of a thicket slept a pretty shepherdess.' We sing with calm and conviction, and we're not mad.

On, on we walk, every step we take is one less to reach home. We cross a village that's bigger than usual, with some houses built in brick. One can see we must be out of the steppes by now. We're entering the Ukraine.

Every now and again a soldier runs into a house and comes out again with a honeycomb. A man in my platoon brings Cenci a pailful of milk and honey. Cenci drinks it greedily. I drink some too and feel as if the drink were turning straight into blood as soon as it gets into me. The road is lined with *isbas* for miles. But most of them are shut, and in the open ones nothing is to be found. Shots sound far away. They may be partisans, and I hurry along the column to reach my company. As I pass by an artillery officer begins insulting me: 'It's always the way with these stragglers. Always the first to run ahead in the clear and always the last when there's a fight on.' He gives me a push. 'I'm from the Vestone,' I said, 'I'm looking for my platoon. Rigoni's my name.' 'You're Rigoni?' says the officer and laughs. He's a Second-Lieutenant in the Vicenza group who'd known me in Albania.

The column has stopped. Major Bracchi and other officers at the head have been shot at by a machine-gun burst. An artillery officer has been wounded in the foot. Bracchi shouts to me to bring up the heavy machine-gun. From a courtyard we fire at Russians running by us. Beside my heavy is an old Fiat gun worked by the artillerymen. They're firing well too. In the courtyard are a lot of high officers watching us. I feel as if I were doing my tests for corporal and blush when the gun, which has sunk into the snow, changes range and fires short.

The Russians go down into a ditch and disappear. The wounded Lieutenant is lying on a table in the *isba* nearby. I can hear him joking with the other officers. The General's there too. A Russian woman brings everyone coffee and gives me a cup. Yet the machine-gun bursts must have come from this very house.

The main part of the column stops in the village and we of the Vestone with an Alpini battery go on towards another village situated on the right above a rise. It's night when we reach it. We enter it cautiously, with sections in extended order, and scatter among the *isbas*. We are comfortable, a platoon per *isba*; and my platoon is reduced from fifty men to less than twenty. We find potatoes, honey, chickens, and prepare our supper light heartedly. We'll have a good evening, it seems, and then a good sleep too.

Rino is in an *isba* near mine, with others from home, Renzo, Adriano, Guzzo. Their unit has been attached to my battalion in place of a company that was taken prisoner. On coming back from visiting them I find supper almost over and the straw already laid for sleep. A young Russian with delicate and noble features is being very helpful: bringing in wood to burn, taking benches and tables outside to make room, preparing plates and spoons. He limps about, drooping with his hands almost touching the ground, laughing continuously. As I watch him Giuanin comes and whispers to me: 'Sergeant-major, the straw outside is full of weapons.' I go out to look. It's quite true. Under a haystack near the *isba* I find automatic weapons and grenades. When we go in again the lame youth has vanished. My companions say he must be quite a good partisan.

It's the 26th of January, that day we've so often talked about. The sun rising from the low horizon is sending out its first rays. The whiteness of the snow and sun is dazzling.

We have some German tanks with us. Far away a sledge is making off at high speed, some shots are fired from a German tank and the sledge blows up. We stop farther on and wait for the main body of the column. From the edge of an escarpment we see below us a big village that looks like a town; Nikolajewka. They say that beyond it is a railway with a train waiting for us. If we reach the railway we'll be out of the bag. We look down and feel that this time it really is true. Meanwhile the main body of the column is nearing us. In the sky appear three or four rather huge aeroplanes, which dive to machine-gun our comrades. We see the spurts of flame from all the guns on board and the column breaking up and scattering. The aeroplanes go along up the column and continue machine-gunning, flying towards the end which is lost like a black line in the steppes.

They say, and go on saying, that at Nikolajewka there are three divisions of Russians. But to judge by the way things have gone, I should say not. The Vestone, the Valchiese, the Edolo, the Tirano are to attack. Our artillery is in position. The Colonel and the General consult maps and then call the battalion commanders in conference. We of the Vestone are to attack on the right. The rendezvous is the square in front of the church. There can't be any artillery preparation because there's very little ammunition. The artillerymen are very disappointed.

I find Rino again, and greet him as if we were on our village square back home. 'Till this evening,' I say, and greet the others from home: 'To it, lads,' I say. 'Keep calm.'

Cenci and Moscioni and I smoke a last cigarette. The Captain inspects us one by one. Finally we move. My platoon is the last on the right. The Captain is between me and Cenci's platoon. Then come the others. As we move out into the open we are at once greeted with anti-tank and mortar fire.

My men hesitate, hold back, one or two of them are already wounded, and I shout: 'Come on.' I too hesitate a bit, but we're in it now, whatever happens. The Captain shouts: 'Forward! Forward!' My comrades begin to follow me, and Antonelli and one or two others pass me. I've got the heavy machine-gun with me, but we haven't any ammunition. Moreschi's section is supposed to bring some. But Moreschi is hanging back a bit and so are his men. I call him: 'Come on down; come on, it's all the same now.' The shots bury themselves in the snow round us. We continue to advance. The Captain is clutching a Russian sub-machine-gun, pointing to the village and shouting: 'Forward! Forward!'

At this moment I think anxiously of Rino, and look round to where his unit is coming down. Now they're firing with machine-guns too; the bullets plunge wailing into the snow and follow us step by step. One or two men are hit and collapse groaning in the snow. But we can't even stop to see who's hit. I shout for them to scatter. But it's useless because when danger's worst the instinct is to do the opposite. The Captain shouts to me to move farther to the right and higher up. There's a slight dip to get over. Then we make a very clear target, with the sun in our faces and the machine-guns en-fillading us. I see Cenci crumple on the snow and hear him shout: 'I'm wounded in both legs.' Two Alpini of his platoon carry him back. They have to return in the open up to the rest of the column. I wonder if they'll get there alive. But he was tough, Cenci was, and I found him in Italy again six months later.

Artico, the senior corporal, takes over command of the platoon at once and shouts to everyone: 'Forward the second and third platoons!' A machine-gun is shooting short, precise bursts at me. 'There,' I think, holding my breath, 'now I'll die.' And I hold my breath; now I'll die. I lie down in a little trough in the snow and the bullets fall round me raising spray. The saliva sticks in my mouth. I don't know what I think or what I'm doing, I look at the sprays of snow a handsbreadth from my head. Antonelli and some others pass me ten yards ahead, and then I get up and go on again.

Looking to the left I see the engineer unit going in to attack an anti-tank gun that was firing at us. After throwing hand-grenades and a short scuffle the gun is taken. These engineers have all the gusto of men in their first battle. It must be because they haven't been in one before. I feel so war-weary compared to them.

We're nearing the railway embankment behind which the Russians are entrenched. Pressing towards the centre with my platoon, I find Sergeant Minelli of Moscioni's platoon; he's losing blood from various light wounds in the head and arms; but his leg has been smashed by an anti-tank shell. He's lamenting and weep-ing: 'I've had it,' he says in Brescian, 'I've had it!' I encourage him as much as I can. 'You're not seriously wounded,' I say. 'Cheer up, Minelli, the stretcher-bearers are behind, they'll come and fetch you.' I'm lying, for God knows where the stretcher-bearers are. Perhaps waiting up there seeing how things go. But Minelli believes me. He waves at me, and even smiles amid his tears. I'd like to stop with him but can't, my men are waiting for me at the embankment and Antonelli is calling me. Minelli begins saying: 'My baby son, my baby son,' and sobbing.

We fire from the edge of the embankment; Moscioni is firing a machine-gun; we fire too with the heavy at some retreating Russians. Behind here we can draw breath a bit; but there are very few of us. Looking back to where we've come down I can see numbers of black spots on the snow. But I know that some of the men in my company have also feigned dead so as not to go into the attack. Now we have to leave our shelter. We fix our bayonets. The Captain is testing his Russian sub-machine-gun, he blows on to the barrel then looks at me: 'Cheer up, lads,' he says, 'it's the last time.' He gives us orders: 'You, Rigoni, go along that way with your men. You,' he says to Moscioni, 'begin going with Rigoni then turn to the left when you're level with that *isba*. Pendoli, with the headquarters platoon, and Artico with the second and third come with me. Let's start.' We scramble across the railway embankment, are greeted by a burst or two but throw ourselves down on the other slope. I don't meet much resistance, the Captain with his two platoons meets more but then that yields too. On my right I notice some Russians dressed in white but do nothing about them and continue to go ahead. Now our artillery is firing too; I see Russians running through the village square.

We leave the wounded in one of the first *isbas*. There's a Russian woman there and I ask her to look after them. I also leave Dotti from Moreschi's section with them. With Antonelli and the heavy machine-gun I enter another *isba*. It seems an excellent place to site the gun. A soldier from my platoon follows me with a case of ammunition. I break a window with the butt of my rifle and drag up to it a table covered with an embroidered cloth. We set the gun up on the table and fire through the window. The Russians are a hundred yards or so away, facing in the other direction. We take them by surprise but have to be careful of our ammunition. While we are firing the children in the *isba* gather sobbing round their mother's skirts. The woman, on the other hand, is calm and serious. She looks silently at us.

During a pause I see a man's boots sticking out from under the bed. I raise the coverlet and make him come out. He's a thin old man who looks at us in terror like a fox in a trap. Antonelli laughs and makes a gesture of kicking him in the backside and I send him to join the woman and children.

We also fire some bursts at a group of Russians who are dragging along an anti-tank gun. Only three belts remain.

We go out of the *isba* and meet Menegolo, who's looking for us with a case of ammunition. I'm annoyed that Moscioni doesn't appear with the other cases. Antonelli and Menegolo site the gun at the corner of an *isba*; I direct their fire from a little ahead to their right and fire my rifle through the cracks of a fence. We're still taking the Russians in the rear and giving them a good deal of bother. I hope meanwhile that the column's decided to move down from where we left it motionless. After we've been firing a bit the Russians succeed in spotting us and an anti-tank shell carries away a corner of the *isba* a few inches above Antonelli's head. 'Let's move,' I shout. But Antonelli strides the tripod and says: 'Now I've really got 'em well sighted.' And goes on firing.

Lieutenant Danda with a few soldiers from the 54th (I think) tries to cross the road and join us, but some shots come from a house near us and he's wounded in an arm.

Our artillery hasn't been firing any more for some time. They hadn't many shells, and will have fired them all. But why doesn't the main body of the column come down? What are they waiting for? We can't go on alone and are already half-way through the village. They could come down almost undisturbed now that we've made the Russians retreat and are keeping them at bay. We don't even know what's happened to the other platoons that attacked with us.

Including Lieutenant Danda's men there must be about twenty of us. What can we do alone? We've scarcely any more ammunition. We've lost touch with the Captain. We haven't any orders. If only we at least had some ammunition! But now I feel hungry too, and the sun's just going down. I cross the fence and a bullet whistles near me. The Russians have their eyes on us. I run and knock at the door of an *isba*, and enter.

There are Russian soldiers there. Prisoners? No. They're armed. With the red stars on their caps. My rifle's in my hand. I look at them, turned to stone. They're eating round a table, taking the food with a wooden spoon from a common bowl. And they look at me with their spoons held in mid-air. '*Mnie khocetsia iestj*,' I say. There are also some women. One takes a plate, fills it with milk and meal and offers it to me with a spoon from the common bowl. I take a step forward, sling my rifle over my shoulder and eat. Time doesn't exist any more. The Russian soldiers look at me. The women look at me. The children look at me. No one breathes a word. The only sound is of the spoon in my plate; and of each of my mouthfuls. '*Spaziba*,' I say when I've finished. And the woman takes the empty bowl from my hands. '*Pas austa*,' she replies simply. The Russian soldiers watch me go out, without moving. There are some beehives in the entrance lobby. The woman who gave me the soup has come with me as if to open the door and I ask her by signs to give me a honeycomb for my companions. She gives me a honeycomb and I go out.

That's how it happened, this incident. Now, thinking it over, I don't find it at all strange, but natural—with that naturalness there must have been between all men at one time. After the first surprise all my gestures were natural. I didn't feel any fear, or any wish to defend myself or to offend them. It was very simple. The Russians were like me too, I felt. In that *isba* there'd been created between me, the Russian soldiers, the women and the children a harmony which wasn't just a truce. It was something much more than the respect which animals in the forest have for each other. Circumstances, just for once, had helped men to remain human. Who knows where those men, those women, those children are now? I hope the war has spared them all. For the rest of our lives we'll all of us, children included, remember how we behaved then. Particularly the children. If it's happened once it might happen again. It might happen again, I mean, with innumerable other men and become a habit, a way of life.

On getting back to my comrades we hang the honeycomb on the branch of a tree and eat it all up, a piece each. Then I look around

as if waking from a dream. The sun is vanishing over the horizon.
I look at the gun and the two remaining belts of cartridges. I look
at the deserted roads of the village and notice a group of armed men
coming towards us. They're dressed in white and walking con-
fidently. Are they ours? Are they Germans? Are they Russians?
When they're about ten yards or so from us they stop and look at us.
They're Russians. I hurriedly order the others to follow me and
fling myself between the *isbas* and the gardens. Antonelli and
Menegolo follow with the gun. They're all looking at me as if they
were expecting a miracle from me. I realize the situation is desperate. But it doesn't occur to me to give up. An Alpino, I don't
know from what company, has a machine-gun but no ammunition;
another comes up and says: 'I've got more than a hundred rounds.'
Peering over a fence I fire a couple of belts from the machine-gun at
a group of Russians not far away and then pass the gun to an Alpino:
'Fire,' I say. The Alpino fires over the fence but then falls with a
groan at my feet, hit in the head. The hundred rounds are already
finished. Antonelli has also finished his ammunition and is now dismembering the heavy machine-gun and burying the pieces in the
snow. So our company loses its last gun.

There are less than twenty of us now. 'Come on,' I say, 'get ready
all you can, then follow me.' We come out from behind the fence.
Although there are only a handful of us we make enough noise for
three times the number and the grenades do the rest. I don't know
if we broke through or if the Russians let us pass; the fact is that
we got away. We reach the railway embankment at a run, and crawl
into a narrow tunnel running underneath it; when I put my head
out the other side I see the snow in front of me covered with bodies.
Bullets graze my nose. 'Back,' I shout, 'back!' We crawl back one
after the other to the other end again. I throw myself into a small
ditch and run along the bottom of it. The others follow. Running
under a hedge I hear the bullets falling just behind us. We reach the
isbas from which they'd been firing at us that morning with anti-
tank guns. There we stop a moment to gather breath and look at
each other. We're still all there. I see Lieutenant Pendoli coming
out of the nearest *isba*. 'Rigoni,' he calls, 'Rigoni, come here and
fetch our Captain who's wounded.' 'What about the others?' I ask.
'Where are they?' 'There aren't any others,' replies Lieutenant

Pendoli. 'Let's go and get the Captain,' I say to my comrades. But now from the *isbas* around, from the thickets, from the gardens, appear dozens of Russian soldiers, firing as they come. Many of my comrades fall, others run towards the little railway embankment, reach it and are met by a hail of fire. Another two or three fall. I rush to join the remainder. The bullets hit the rails like a hailstorm and sparks fly, but I manage to roll over to the other side. The few others who've escaped are floundering over the snow. The embankment is between us and the Russians. I pass near an anti-tank gun and stop to try and take the breech-block out to make it unserviceable. But meanwhile the Russians appear on the embankment and are at me. Then I begin running uphill ahead as best I can, continually sinking to my knees in the snow. I'm quite open to the Russian fire and every step I take a bullet reaches near me. 'Now's the time to die,' I say to myself, like a record repeating itself. 'Now's the time to die. Now's the time to die.'

I hear someone groaning and begging for help and go up to him. It's an Alpino who was in our stronghold on the Don. He's wounded in the legs and stomach with anti-tank shrapnel. I put my arms under his shoulders and drag him along. But it's too difficult and I try to carry him. The Russians are firing an anti-tank gun at us. I sink into the snow, take a step forward, fall down and the Alpino groans. I haven't the strength to go on carrying him, but manage to get him to some kind of shelter. Anyway the Russians have stopped firing. I tell the Alpino to try to walk. He tries, fails, and we stop behind a heap of manure. 'Stay here,' I say, 'I'll send a sledge for you. And cheer up, you're not seriously wounded.'

Afterwards I forgot to send a sledge for him, but our company stretcher-bearers passed that way and collected him. Later in Italy I heard he'd been saved and a great weight fell from me. When it was all over I met him one day at Brescia. I didn't recognize him, but he saw me from far away, ran towards me and embraced me: 'Don't you remember, Sergeant-major?' I didn't recognize him and looked at him. 'Don't you remember?' he repeated, and knocked his hand against his wooden leg. 'Don't you remember the 26th of January?' Then I remembered and we embraced each other again with the crowds around watching us, not understanding what it was all about.

As I go walking on alone over the snow, I suddenly hear a noise and see the black mass of the column come rushing down the slope. What the hell are they doing? They'll be exterminated by the Russian fire. Why didn't they come down before? There are the aeroplanes again. They're firing and dropping incendiaries. It's like this morning all over again. There's also anti-tank and mortar fire from the village. Some German tanks are going down, slowly and carefully. One is hit and stops, but continues to fire its gun. The others pass near me. They're followed by groups of German soldiers, and I join them. So, firing our rifles from behind the tanks, we reach the first houses again. I try by signs to get a tank to go where our wounded Captain is, giving them to understand he's a senior officer. After much hesitation the Germans yield to my insistence. We go a few yards in the direction I'm pointing and then an anti-tank shell fractures the periscope. The tank is forced to stop and we have to give up. There aren't enough of us to get into the village without tank support.

Meanwhile night has come on. From behind a ruined house I fire at the Russians who're passing among the gardens. Now I'm alone. Twenty yards to the right a German soldier is dragging himself cautiously over the snow towards two Russians who are in position behind a wall. Then he throws two grenades at them. I run behind a house farther on. From the pavement in front a Russian soldier sees me and turns to aim at me. We exchange rifle shots, I from my shelter and he from his. A Captain of Alpino artillery comes towards me and falls hit in the chest just as he's about to say something to me. His blood spurts out over my boots and socks. His batman arrives. Another officer arrives. They lean over him as he groans. Then as soon as he's dead the batman takes the wallet from his pocket and the gold watch from his wrist. I'm exhausted and go and sit behind a little hedge. A Second-Lieutenant comes up to me shouting: 'Coward, what are you doing there? Come on out.' I don't even look at him, and finally he too sits down beside me and even stays there after I've gone.

He tells me that Lieutenant-Colonel Calbo of the artillery has been hit. I go and look for him. His batman is holding his head up and sobbing. The Colonel's eyes are veiled and perhaps he can't see any more. He talks to me thinking I'm Major Bracchi. I don't remember what he said; I only remember the sound of his voice, the gasping due to his wound, and he lying on the snow. There was something grandiose in his appearance and I felt timid and bewildered. Meanwhile the German tanks have begun advancing again. Alpini and Germans get behind them. The bullets fall on the tanks' armour and glance off towards us. Crouching on one tank and shouting encouragement at us is General Reverberi. Then he gets down and walks alone in front of the tanks waving his pistol.

Insistent fire is coming from a house. Just from one house. 'Are there any officers there?' the General shouts towards us. There may be some officers, but none of them come out. 'Any Alpini?' he shouts again. A group of us comes out from behind the tanks. 'Go to that house and stop them,' he says. We go and the Russians leave.

Now it's night, the column has returned to the village and everyone is looking for a place to spend a warm night, and if possible eat something. The confusion now! It's like a fair. I meet some engineers and ask them about Rino. They'd seen him slightly wounded in the shoulder during the first assault and know nothing since then. I call and search for him without finding him. Then with Captain Marcolini and Lieutenant Zanotelli from my battalion I stand near the church and we shout: 'Vestone! Vestone! On parade, Vestone!' But how can the dead reply? 'D'you remember, Rigoni, the first of September?' says the Lieutenant sobbing, 'it's like that.' 'It's worse,' I say.

Our shouts are answered by Baroni of the mortars, who comes up with a little group from his platoon. They still have a mortar, but no bombs, nothing else. From the whole of the Vestone we manage to collect about thirty men. The *isbas* are all full and we get into the school. But the windows are broken, there's no straw and the floor's made of cement. We lie down but it's impossible to sleep. We're freezing. An Alpino from my company whom we called 'the old hag,' has found some biscuits somewhere or other and gives me one. We munch them together. Bodei, who's near me, is trembling with cold. We get up and go out. I knock at an *isba*; a German soldier comes to the door with his pistol at the ready and points it at my chest. 'I want to come in,' I say. Gently I push the pistol aside with one hand and laugh in his face. He's so surprised he puts it back in his holster and shuts the door behind me. We go into a

stall and light a small fire with twigs. We warm ourselves, but the
side which doesn't face the fire is frozen stiff. The mules look at us
with their ears down, and their heads swaying from side to side.
Slowly I fall asleep with my back leaning against a stake.

That was the 26th of January 1943. My dearest friends left me
that day.

Of Rino, who'd been wounded during the first attack, I never
managed to get any definite news. His mother is still waiting for
him, it's all she lives for. I see her every day when I pass her door.
Her eyes are sunken. Every time she sees me she almost cries and I
haven't the courage to talk to her. Raul left me that day too. Raul,
the first friend I made in the army. He was on a tank and as he
jumped down to go on still a little nearer home, a burst caught him
and he died on the snow. Raul, who always used to sing, 'Good
night, my love,' before going to sleep. And who once, at the ski-ing
course, made me almost cry reading *The Lament of the Madonna* by
Jacopone da Todi. Giuanin's dead too. There you are, Giuanin,
you've reached home. We'll all reach it. Giuanin died while he was
carrying the ammunition for our heavy machine-gun and I was
firing it. He died on the snow, he who in the dugout had always felt
cold and was always crouching in his niche near the stove. The
chaplain of the battalion also died: 'Happy Christmas, lads, and
peace be with you.' He died going to fetch a wounded man under
fire. 'Be calm now and write home.' 'Happy Christmas, padre.' And
the Captain's dead too. The smuggler of Valstagna. He got a bullet
right through his chest. The drivers that night put him on a sledge
and carried him out of the bag. He died in hospital at Kharkov.
When I got back in the spring I went to his home. I walked through
the woods and the valleys. 'Hallo? Valstagna here, Beppo speaking.
How are things?' And his home was old and rustic, clean as Lieutenant Cenci's dugout. And how many others from my platoon and my
strongpoint died that day? We must always stick together, lads,
even now. Lieutenant Moscioni got a hole in his shoulder and the
wound wouldn't heal even in Italy. Now the wound's healed but
not other things. Oh, no, they can't heal. And General Martinat
died that day. I remember when I accompanied him along our lines
in Albania. I'd hurried on ahead of him because I knew the way and
looked back to see if he was following me. 'Go on, go on, as fast as

you like, Corporal, I've got good legs too.' And Colonel Calbo also, who was so good with his artillery, the 19th and the 20th. And Sergeant Minelli was also wounded on the snow there: 'I've had it,' he said and wept, 'I've had it.' Giuanin, too few of us have reached home, after all. Not even Moreschi has returned. 'Have you ever seen a seven-hundredweight goat?' 'Always filthy Macedonias!' Nor has Pintossi, the old sportsman, reached home to shoot his native game again. His old dog will be dead too by now. So many, so many others are sleeping in the wheat fields among the butterflies and the flowering grasses of the steppes, together with the old men of Gorki's and Gogol's stories. And the few of us who've remained, where are we now?

When I woke up I found my boots had burnt. I heard sounds of people getting ready for departure. I couldn't find anyone from my company or battalion. In the dark I'd even lost Bodei, and was left alone. I tried to walk on as fast as I could, for the Russians might try and catch us again. It was still night and there was a great noise going on all over the village. Wounded groaned on the snow and in the *isbas*. But now I thought of nothing any more; not even of home. I was arid as a stone and swept along like a stone by the current. I never bothered to look for my companions or even after a time, to walk fast. Just like a stone carried along by the current. Nothing made an impression any more. If there'd been another battle I'd have gone into it, but on my own; without caring who followed or overtook me. I'd have gone through it on my own; personally; isolated; from *isba* to *isba*, from garden to garden; without listening to orders, or giving them, free of everything, like on a mountain shoot; alone.

I still had a dozen rifle rounds and three hand-grenades. Few others in the column, perhaps, had as much ammunition as I had.

Another day of walking over the snow. My burnt boots are falling to pieces and I've tied them to my feet with bits of wire and rags. The hard leather had broken the skin underneath and formed an open wound. My knees ache; they go crick-crack at every step I take. Dysentery's also coming over me. I walk on for miles and miles without saying a word to anyone.

Now the column is proceeding in scattered groups. The strongest are walking quickly, the others following as best they can. I'm not

so many battles, that fired so well and that I was so fond of. Who'd taken it off me?

The officers had gone, I can't say they had taken it. But that's what I think. I was sorry, really sorry about it. Now that we were out of the bag the ones without arms, who were the most numerous, were trying to take the arms off those who'd kept them up to now. I would not and could not return unarmed to my companions. I'd already thrown away my helmet, anti-gas mask and pack, burnt my boots, lost my gloves, but my old rifle I'd always kept with me. I still had the cartridge-belts and hand-grenades. In the *isba* was a heavy, clumsy old rifle. I took that; the cartridges fitted. When I went out I heard shots and shouting near the village. Partisans or regular soldiers were attacking the last stragglers in the column. So's not to be taken prisoner I ran as fast as I could between the gardens and the *isbas*, behind the fences and then into the steppe until I finally rejoined the column.

The wound on my foot had gone poisoned and stank, I could smell it as I walked and the sock was sticking to it. It hurt; it felt as if someone had plunged their teeth into my foot and wouldn't move them. My knees creaked; at every step they went crick-crack. I was walking steadily but slowly, and even by forcing myself couldn't get along faster. I'd found a stick in a garden and leant on that.

Another night I stopped in an *isba* where there was a medical Lieutenant being helped by a Ukrainian guard (one of those civilians with a white armband who worked with the occupation troops). The Ukrainian was preparing some broth of millet and milk and gave me a plateful. It was really good. I took off the rags and broken boots. The sock was sticking to the wound and the smell of decay was really foul. Around the wound the flesh was whitish, or rather dirty yellow. I washed it with salt and water, wrapped it in a piece of cloth, put on the socks and the remains of the boots and tied them together with bits of wire.

In that village the evening before, I'd met Renzo. 'How's it go, friend?' I asked him. 'All right,' he replied. 'All right. Look, I'm in that *isba* there; tomorrow we'll leave together,' and he hurried away. I saw him again in Italy. I was alone, I didn't need anyone, I wanted to stay alone. Then a German came and knocked at the *isba*. I saw he wasn't like the usual ones. He came in among us and ate with us. Afterwards, sitting on a bench, he took his photographs out of his wallet: 'This is my wife,' he said, 'and this my daughter.' The wife was young and the daughter was a baby. 'And this is my home,' he said then. It was a house in Bavaria, among the firs, in a little village.

For yet another day I walked on, leaning on my stick like an old tramp. For hours I surprised myself repeating, 'Now's the time I'll die,' and this thought went in rhythm with each step. Along the track were numbers of mule carcasses. One day I was cutting myself a hunk of meat off one of these when I heard myself called. It was a senior Corporal of the Verona battalion who'd been a pupil of mine on a mountaineering course in Piedmont. He called me and I saw he was pleased to meet me. 'Shall we walk along together?' he said. 'All right. Come,' I said.

I walked with him for two or three days. At the mountaineering course they'd called him Romeo because one night he'd gone to visit a shepherd girl and climbed in at her window. (It was useful, that course.) They called him Romeo and her Juliet. He was a new recruit and we used to tease him about this. Another evening when we were in a hut high up in the ice he went down to the village and walked the whole night to see her. The next morning we had to climb a peak and he was tired but Lieutenant Suitner loaded him with ropes and equipment. Now here in Russia I'd heard he was one of the best senior Corporals in the Verona. I didn't talk to him much as we walked, but in the evening, when we arrived at the *isbas*, we helped each other to prepare something to eat and to fetch straw to sleep on.

The sun was beginning to make itself felt, the days were getting longer. We were walking along a valley by a river-bed. People said we were out of the bag now and that one of these days we'd be entering the German lines. Those who had been lagging at the end of the column said that every now and again Russian soldiers, tanks and partisans were attacking the stragglers and taking prisoners.

One day, passing a ditch, we saw sledges full of wounded stuck in the snow. Romeo and I were walking outside the track on our own. The driver and wounded of one of the sledges called out for help. There were lots of others round them but they seemed to me to be asking us in particular. I stopped, looked back a little and then went on walking. Afterwards I turned round again, and saw that the sledges had started moving. I was alone, didn't need anyone, didn't want anything.

One day we passed through a village; the sun was still high. At the windows of an *isba* women were tapping on the glass and signing for us to enter. 'Shall we go in?' my companion asks. 'Let's go in,' I say. It's a fine *isba* with embroidered curtains on the windows and ikons decorated with paper flowers. Everything is clean and warm. The women put two chickens on to boil for us, gave us soup to drink, and meat with boiled potatoes. Afterwards we get ready to sleep. Towards evening some N.C.O.'s of the Edolo come in. I ask them about Raul; just on the chance, as I see from their flashes that they're from his battalion. 'He's dead,' they reply, 'he died at Nikolajewka. He was going in to the attack on a tank and as he jumped to the ground a burst got him.' I say nothing.

When I take the first steps next morning I have to move slowly. Crick-crack, go my knees. Very gradually they warm up and then I go on walking, leaning on the stick. My companion is patient and stays silently with me. We're like two old tramps who've joined forces without knowing each other.

Now one often hears curses and quarrels in the column. We've become touchy, nervy, pick on any little thing.

One day we go into a shack, from which we'd heard a cock crow. There are lots of hens in there, and we take one each. We pluck them as we walk along so's to eat them that night. A German Storck plane has landed near the column: some wounded are loaded into it. In a few hours they'll be in hospital. But nothing matters to me any more.

We meet some German soldiers who weren't with us. They're from a strongpoint and were expecting us. They're clean and ordered. One of their officers is scanning the horizon around through binoculars. We're out, I try to think. But I don't feel any excitement even when we pass some road signs written in German.

A General is standing at the side of the track. It's Nasci, the commander of the Alpini corps. Yes, it's really him, with his hand at the peak of his cap, saluting us as we pass. Us, band of scarecrows.

We pass in front of the old man, with his grey moustache. We're in rags, filthy, with long beards, many without boots, frost-bitten, wounded. That old man with the Alpini cap on salutes us. And I feel as if I were seeing my grandfather again.

They're Italian lorries down there, they're our Fiats and our Bianchis. We're out, it's over. They've come to meet us to load up the wounded and the frost-bitten or anyone else who wants to jump on. I look at the trucks and pass them. My wound stinks, my knees ache, but I go on walking on the snow. Notices point: 9th Alpini; 5th Alpini; 2nd Alpini artillery; Verona Battalion (my companion goes off without my even noticing it); Tirano Battalion; Edolo Battalion; Valmonica group. The column is thinning out. 6th Alpini, Vestone Battalion, an arrow points. Am I from the 6th Alpini? From the Vestone Battalion? This way then. Vestone, Vestone, *el Vestù*. My comrades. 'Sergeant-major, shall we ever get home?' I'm home. Now and at the time of our death. 'Rigoni! *Ciao*, Rigoni!' But who's that? Yes, it's Bracchi. He comes towards me, puts a hand on my shoulder. He has washed, shaved. 'Go down there, old man, you'll find your company in those *isbas*.' I look and say nothing. Slowly, very slowly I go down towards the *isbas*. There are three of them. In the first are the drivers with seven mules, in the second the company and in the third another company. I open the door, some Alpini are shaving and washing in the first room. I look round. 'And the others?' I say. 'Sergeant-major! Sergeant-major!' 'Rigoni has arrived too,' they shout. 'And the others?' I repeat. There's Tourn and Bodei, Antonelli and Tardivel. Faces I had forgotten. 'So it's all over then?' I say. They're pleased to see me again and something moves far down inside me like a bubble of air coming from the depths of the sea. 'Come,' says Antonelli. And he accompanies me into the other room where there's an officer who was in the headquarters platoon. 'It's he who's in command of the company,' says Antonelli. The Quartermaster's also there and he notes my name on a piece of paper. 'You're the twenty-seventh,' he says. 'Are you tired, Rigoni?' the Lieutenant asks me. 'Settle down somewhere if you want to rest.'

I throw myself under a table against a wall and curl up there. The whole day and the whole of the following night I stay under there listening to the voices of my companions and watching the feet moving on the beaten earth floor.

In the morning I go out and Tourn brings me a little coffee in the cover of a mess-tin. 'How d'you feel, Sergeant-major?' 'Oh, Tourn! It really is you? And the others?' I say. 'They're here,' he says, 'come.' 'The platoon, our heavy platoon. Where are they?' 'Come along, Sergeant-major.' I call Antonelli, Bodei and one or two others. 'Giuanin,' I ask, 'where is Giuanin?' They say nothing. 'Shall we ever get home?' I ask after Giuanin again. 'He's dead,' Bodei says to me. 'Here's his wallet.' 'And the others?' I ask. 'Including you there are seven of us,' says Antonelli. 'Including you seven from the heavy platoon; and that recruit,' he points to Bosio, 'has a broken leg.' 'And you, Tourn? Show me your hand,' I say. Tourn spreads out his hand. 'You see,' he says, 'it's healed, you see how clean the scar is.' 'If you want to shave and wash I'll go and heat some water,' says Bodei. 'But it doesn't matter, why?' I reply. 'You stink,' Antonelli says to me.

Someone puts a safety-razor and a little mirror into my hand. I look at these things and then look at myself in the glass; so this is me; Mario Rigoni son of Giovan Battista, N. 15454, Sergeant-major of the 6th Alpini regiment, Vestone Battalion, 55th company, machine-gun platoon. A crust of earth on my face, a beard like wisps of straw, moustache filthy with mucus, eyes yellow, hair stuck to the top of my balaclava, a louse walking on my neck. I smile at myself.

Bodei gives me a pair of scissors, I cut most of my beard off and then wash myself. The water comes off me earth-coloured. With the safety-razor, slowly, because God knows how many beards like mine this blade has cut, I begin to shave myself. I leave a little beard on my chin and moustaches like I once wore. Then I wash again and my companions watch me as if I were coming out of a cocoon. Tourn passes me a comb. Oh, how it hurts to comb myself. 'You still stink,' says Antonelli. 'It's my foot,' I say, 'it's my foot. Have you a little salt?' 'There's even salt,' says Bodei. And he boils up some salt and water. 'Are you frost-bitten?' they ask me. I take off the last pieces of boots and rag. What a smell! There seem to be worms in the wound, it's so putrid and foul. I wash it well with salt and water, and my whole feet too. Antonelli has a piece of lint left over from his first-aid kit and binds me up. Finally I go back under the table and stay there gazing fixedly at the walls of the *isba*.

Three days we stayed there. In those three days one or two stragglers arrived. But it was all over now. The Sergeant who had frost-bite left for hospital the day after my arrival. There wasn't a single officer of the company left; Moscioni, Cenci, Pendoli, Signori. Not one and no N.C.O.'s except the Second-Lieutenant and the Sergeant-major of the transport. I loaded Bosio, the recruit from Moreschi's old platoon, who had a wounded leg, on a mule and put him on to a lorry that was taking off the wounded. Another Alpino of the 3rd rifle platoon, who came from Tourn's home parts, was there, wearing a handkerchief round his head. 'What've you got there?' I asked him. He took off the handkerchief and I saw he was without an eye; in its place was a red hole. 'It's healed up now,' he said, 'I'm coming to Italy with you.'

One of those days our Colonel, Signorini, died. They said that after having listened to his battalion commanders' reports and heard what was left of his regiment he retired to a room in the *isba* where he was living and died of a heart attack. I remember him coming to see us one day when we were digging trenches, before we went to the strongpoint on the Don, Bracchi called me and introduced me to the Colonel. As he put his hand on my shoulder his glove caught in a star on my coat and tore. I remember my embarrassment and his smile. And now he's left us too.

I also went to Regimental Headquarters to ask after Marco of the Nogare. 'He's got frost-bite,' they told me, 'and has left for Italy.'

The Lieutenant who'd taken over command of the company asked me the names of those who deserved decorations. I gave the names of Antonelli, Artico, Cenci, Moscioni, Menegolo, Giuanin, Tardivel, and one or two others.

There, now the story of the bag is finished, but only of the bag. We still walked for days and days. From the Ukraine to the Polish borders, in White Russia. The Russians continued to advance. Sometimes we made long marches at night too. One day I almost lost my hand from frost-bite because I'd hung on to a lorry and wasn't wearing gloves. There was still torturing snow and cold. We walked along unit by unit, in groups. At night we stopped at *isbas* to sleep and eat. There are so many more things to tell, but that would be another story.

One day I realized that spring had arrived. We'd been walking for so many days; it seemed our fate to walk. And I noticed that the snow was melting, that there were puddles in the villages we passed. The sun was warm, one could hear a lark sing. A lark singing for the spring. I longed to stretch out on green grass and hear the wind between the branches of the fir-trees. And water gurgling between stones.

In White Russia, near Gomel, we waited for the train that was to take us back to Italy. Our company, only a handful now, was in a village near the forest. To reach it we had to walk some hours through the melting snowfields. The place was famous for partisans; not even the Germans dared go there. They sent us. The *starosta* of the village told us that we must distribute ourselves in ones or twos to each family so as not to burden the population. The *isba* where they accepted me was spacious and clean, and lived in by a family of simple young peasants. I made myself a place to sleep in a corner under the window. The whole time I was in that house I spent lying on some straw; always there, lying for hours and hours looking at the ceiling. In the afternoons there was only a girl and new-born baby in the *isba*. The girl sat near the cradle. The cradle hung from the ceiling by ropes and swayed to and fro every time the baby moved. I looked at the ceiling and the sound of the spinning-wheel filled my being like the sound of some enormous waterfall. Sometimes I would watch it, and the March sun, coming through the curtains, made the flax seem like gold, as the spinning-wheel squeaked away. Every now and again the baby cried and then the girl would rock the cradle gently and sing. I listened and never said a word. Some afternoons her friends came in from the houses nearby. They'd bring their spinning-wheels and spin with her. They spoke to each other gently, in low voices, as if afraid of disturbing me. Their voices were harmonious and the whir of the spinning-wheel made them sweeter than ever. This was my cure. They also sang; the old songs they'd always sung; *Stienka Rasin, Natalka Poltawka* and their ancient dance tunes. I would look at the ceiling for hours and hours and listen. In the evening they called me to come and eat with them. They all ate from the same dish, with quiet concentration. The mother would return; the father would return; the boy would return. The father and the boy only returned in the evening; they didn't stop for long, every now and again they'd look out of the window, then go out together until the next evening. One evening when they didn't come the girl wept. They returned in the morning . . . The baby slept in its wooden cradle, which swung gently from the ceiling; the sun came in through the window and made the flax like gold: the spinning-wheel whirred and flashed; it was like a waterfall; and amid the sound the girl's voice was slow and sweet.